The New Frugality

By the same author

Right on the Money: Taking Control of Your Personal Finances

Deflation: What Happens When Prices Fall?

The New Frugality

How to Consume Less, Save More, and Live Better

Chris Farrell

BLOOMSBURY PRESS
New York Berlin London

Published by Bloomsbury Press, New York

All papers used by Bloomsbury Press are natural, recyclable products made from wood grown in well-managed forests. The manufacturing processes conform to the environmental regulations of the country of origin.

LIBRARY OF CONGRESS CATALOGING-IN-PUBLICATION DATA

Farrell, Chris.
  The new frugality : how to consume less, save more, and live better / Chris Farrell.—1st U.S. ed.
      p. cm.
  Includes index.
  ISBN-13: 978-1-59691-660-9 (hardcover : alk. paper)
  ISBN-10: 1-59691-660-5 (hardcover : alk. paper)
  1. Finance, Personal.   2. Saving and investment.   I. Title.
  HG179.F363 2010
  332.024—dc22

                                                           2009030375

This publication is designed to provide accurate and authoritative information in regard to the subject matter covered. It is published with the understanding that the publisher and author are not engaged in rendering legal, accounting, or other professional service. If legal advice or other professional advice, including financial, is required, the services of a competent professional person should be sought.

First U.S. Edition 2010

3 5 7 9 10 8 6 4 2

Designed by Rachel Reiss

Typeset by Westchester Book Group
Printed in the United States of America by Worldcolor Fairfield

To Mom and Dad

*This time, like all times, is a very good one, if we but
know what to do with it . . . Finish each day and be done
with it. You have done what you could. Some blunders and
absurdities no doubt crept in; forget them as soon as you can.
Tomorrow is a new day; begin it well and serenely and with
too high a spirit to be encumbered with your old nonsense.*
—Ralph Waldo Emerson

Contents

Acknowledgments

I owe an enormous debt of gratitude to many people. I'd like to thank Suzanne Woolley, senior editor in the personal-finance department at *BusinessWeek*. She's a wonderful editor, a constant source of insight and cheer. She helped me immensely with the book. Michael Mandel, chief economist at *BusinessWeek*, is a friend and fount of ideas that influenced the shape of this book. Mark Alfuth, chief financial officer at American Public Media, carefully went through the manuscript with me. His advice was invaluable. Stephen Smith, executive editor and host of American RadioWorks at American Public Media, is a good friend and colleague, always wise in counsel, with a knack for knowing when it's time for some humor. He also wields a good red pencil. I received perceptive comments on a rough work in progress from Peter Clowney, Laurie Stern, Ron Jepperson, Robert Barker, and Lisa Kane.

Marketplace Money is a one-hour personal-finance show nationally syndicated by APM. I learned a lot from a terrific group of colleagues, host Tess Vigeland, senior producer Deborah Clark, and assistant producers Stephen Hoffman and Eve Troeh. J. J. Yore, vice president of programming and executive producer at *Marketplace*, cheerfully supported the project (occasionally shaking his head and saying, "If you really want to do this to yourself . . ."). I'm grateful for the support of APM, especially Bill Kling, Jon McTaggart, Judy McAlpine, and Kate Moos.

There are so many people that I'd like to thank for their counsel and ideas about personal finance over the years. I can't list them all, but there are a few I'd like to highlight. Among the financiers that have instructed me are Professor Zvi Bodie of Boston University, Professor Meir Statman of Santa Clara University, Professor Burton Malkiel of Princeton University, and Professor Jeremy Siegel of the Wharton School. In addition, I am indebted to Jack Bogle, the founder of Vanguard; Ross Levin, certified financial planner and head of the financial-planning firm Accredited Investors; Ruth Hayden, financial educator at Ruth L. Hayden Associates; Eric Tyson, personal-finance author; and Michael Mauboussin, chief investment strategist at Legg Mason Capital Management. A special thanks to the late Peter Bernstein, economic historian and philosopher of risk.

I am extremely lucky to work with the book agent Joelle Delbourgo. Thanks to Peter Ginna, publisher at Bloombury Press and Pete Beatty, associate editor at Bloomsbury. I enjoyed their editing and comments. They managed to stay cheerful and supportive even as deadlines were missed.

The only reason I even had the opportunity to write this book was the medical care I got after being diagnosed with colon cancer in spring 2007. Following colon surgery and six months of chemo, I'm doing well. I can't sing the praises enough of the nurses and doctors at Abbot Northwestern Hospital and Minnesota Oncology. Primary-care physician Scott Flaata, surgeon Dr. Karim Alavi, oncologist Dr. Burton Schwartz, nutritionist Lisa Kane, and all the nurses and doctors that treated me, thank you.

Finally, I'd like to thank the two best young men I know and love, my sons, Peter and Connor.

CHAPTER 1

The Rise of the New Frugality

A dollar is not value, but representative of value, and at last,
of moral values ... Wealth is mental; wealth is moral.
                                        —Ralph Waldo Emerson

I'M A CARD-CARRYING OPTIMIST, BUT IT had been a rough patch in February 2009. It was cold, which isn't surprising since I live in Minnesota and during winter a slight pall of gloom touches everyone living on the frozen tundra. Even Garrison Keillor, the radio bard of *A Prairie Home Companion,* seemed more Lutheran-tinged depressed than usual during his shows in St. Paul. But the "February in America" pessimism ran far deeper than the weather and season.

The stock market kept hitting new bear-market lows. Companies were laying off workers at a dismaying rate. Colleagues at American Public Media, the St. Paul–based public-radio programming behemoth, were coming by my office worried about their jobs and retirement savings. More listeners than ever were seeking financial advice from *Marketplace Money,* the nationally syndicated public-radio show I work on as economics editor and financial adviser. Many of the stories were heartbreaking: a foreclosed home; a small business gone belly-up; an aged parent struggling to get by on a shrunken portfolio; a college graduate with no job and lots of student loans. And my car was making strange noises. I knew an expensive bill lay in my near future.

In other words, it was time for a beer. I headed off to the Local, an Irish pub in downtown Minneapolis, a favorite spot of mine. The beer came, and it tasted good. I can't really say why, but, one eye on a televised sporting event, I started thinking about an afternoon with my dad toward the end of his life. Tall, with broad shoulders, he had a big Irish head with white hair, and an erect, military bearing. Of course, that's how I remember him.

But that day he was eighty-three years old and frail in Georgetown University Hospital. His leg had been amputated. The surgery hadn't gone well, and the end was near. My mom, my oldest son, and I sat around his hospital bed. Normally reticent, he reflected on his life with an occasional prompt from my mom. He talked about his grandparents' leaving Ireland and illegally entering the United States by walking across the Canadian border; growing up in the Irish section of Yonkers, New York, in the Depression; running aground in the Red Sea during World War II as a navy midshipman; the naval battle of Leyte Gulf near the Philippines; surviving a kamikaze attack; running spies into Eastern Europe and Russia during the Cold War; and the mob on the waterfront. Some of his stories I had heard before, but much of it was new to me. What was comfortably familiar was his laughing so hard at times that tears came.

For us sitting around the hospital bed, it was like listening to a reading of a novel, except it was all true. Still, what I've carried with me ever since is the moment when he looked at us and said matter-of-factly, "I've lived a good life."

He was right, and remembering that, I wasn't gloomy anymore. But not until that evening at the Local did I realize just how much he had influenced me when it comes to my attitude toward money. He had lived through a depression and many recessions as well as long economic booms and bull markets. He had served in two wars and was involved in several other conflicts, was married happily for more than half a century and raised four kids, enjoyed twelve grandchildren, loved his career in the navy and shipping. Dad also had his setbacks and grief, such as losing a daughter to breast cancer.

Here's the thing: Through it all I never remember him succumbing to the dirge of the apocalypse popular during busts or the siren song of a new era during booms. He wasn't cheap. He wasn't extravagant. He saved, took calculated risks, provided a home, educated his children, enjoyed his money, and gave back to the community. He lived "a good life."

The Money Head Fake

We all know that managing money takes time and effort. It's easy to get lost in personal finance poring over 401(k) statements and life insurance policies, struggling to figure out whether it's smarter to set up a traditional IRA or a Roth IRA. It's tough to resist speculative manias when it seems that everyone else is making money. It's also hard to avoid the paralyzing pull of fear when the economy turns down and the unemployment rate surges higher.

Yet a conversation about personal finance is actually something of a "head fake." The term is from a lecture given in the fall of 2007 by Randy Pausch, the Carnegie Mellon computer scientist. It was a humorous, moving talk entitled "Really Achieving Your Childhood Dreams." During the lecture Pausch openly discussed the pancreatic cancer that would kill him in less than a year. The talk became an Internet phenomenon. Here's an example he gave of a head fake: "When we send our kids out to play football or soccer or swimming or whatever it is . . . we actually don't want our kids to learn football. I mean, it's really nice that I have a wonderful three-point stance . . . But we send our kids out to learn much more important things: teamwork, sportsmanship, perseverance."

In other words, a head fake is when it seems we're learning one thing, yet we're actually gaining a different—and far more important—type of knowledge.

What's the head fake when it comes to personal finance? I'll discuss a number of critical and classic money topics, such as investing in stocks, getting out of credit card debt, and taking out student loans. Yet personal finance is really about deciding how to live your life, figuring out what you really cherish and value, then putting your money behind those goals and beliefs. It's about trying to create a good life. That's the spirit and the purpose informing this book.

The New Frugality

The Great Recession marks a major inflection point in managing our money. Our love affair with consumer debt is over. The embrace of what I'm calling the New Frugality signals that half a century of people spending with abandon and borrowing as much as possible is done. Profligacy is out. Frugality is in. We've already made dramatic strides. Government statistics show that the personal savings rate is up sharply from its near zero level in 2007. "The country has drifted away from the concept of thrift to our detriment," says Robert Frank, economist at Cornell University. "We are clearly talking about the end of the consuming generation of reckless spenders," says Henry "Bud" Hebeler, formerly president of Boeing's aerospace unit and now a passionate proselytizer for sensible financial planning.

The change toward saving runs deep. The painful lesson of two recessions, two bear markets, a credit crunch, and a government bailout of the financial system in less than a decade is that job and income insecurity is a part of everyday life. A generation has learned the hard way the dangers of borrowing too much. The turn toward financial conservatism will be reinforced by anemic income growth and weakened household balance sheets. It will be a long time before the battered financial system is healthy enough to lend freely.

The New Frugality Embraces a Margin of Safety

The New Frugality means accepting the wisdom of always managing our finances with a "margin of safety" in mind. In practical terms, creating a margin of safety is siphoning more of our earnings into savings, paying off debts, and borrowing less. A healthy financial buffer offers shelter against terrifying downturns in the economy and upheavals in the financial markets. It's a household money cushion against life's inevitable setbacks, such as a layoff or medical illness. The security part of the margin-of-safety equation will dominate our thinking over the next few years with disturbing memories of the Great Recession still fresh.

But a margin of safety involves much more than taking out an insurance policy against tragedy and trauma. By finding the right balance between caution and boldness, a margin of safety allows for sensible risk taking over a lifetime. A healthy household balance sheet lets us pursue intriguing opportunities when they come along, to take risks that might lead to a more satisfying career, to embrace changes in our lives that

 Here are examples of managing money with a margin-of-safety approach.

A down payment of 20 percent or more on a home

A thirty-year fixed-rate mortgage

An emergency savings fund covering twelve months or more of expenses

Spending less than you earn

Earning a college diploma

Paying off the credit card bill in full

Life insurance for your family

Disability insurance for work

Saving for retirement

could lead to greater happiness. Safety and opportunity, like risk and re-turn, are two sides of the margin-of-safety coin.

The New Frugality Is Sustainable

This is also the age of global warming and sustainability. My premise is that sustainability will powerfully influence the economics of everyday money management. The New Frugality reflects a growing embrace of a sustainability ethic or outlook. The sustainability concern about trying to reduce our impact on the planet's ecology without harming future genera-tions is no longer largely limited to environmentalists, climate scientists, and community activists. It is moving from society's tributaries into the mainstream of American business and government, college campuses, and ordinary neighborhoods. Climate change affects all of us. The underlying science is well established.

What is sustainability? In many respects, it's an amorphous, am-biguous term with many shades of meaning. The most common defini-tions are often jargon-laden laundry lists agreed to after long negotiations at international conferences. Still, a few common themes are concern for the planet's ecology; awareness of global warming; the desire to cut down on waste; worries over the viability of local communities; and eq-uity between generations. For an attitude toward managing personal fi-nances, my favorite definition comes from the late actor and nonprofit entrepreneur Paul Newman: "We are such spendthrifts with our lives. The trick of living is to slip on and off the planet with the least fuss you can muster. I'm not running for sainthood. I just happen to think that in life we need to be a little like the farmer, who puts back into the soil what he takes out."

That sounds about right to me. But for our purposes, what's important · is how in everyday money decisions, being frugal and being green are synonymous. Over time, experience will demonstrate that a sustainable sensibility both saves money and does good. The core of my argument is that the sustainability message of conservative consumerism and the

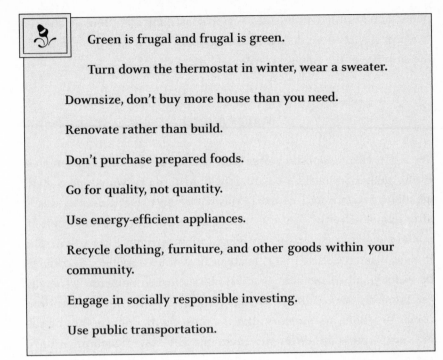

Green is frugal and frugal is green.

Turn down the thermostat in winter, wear a sweater.

Downsize, don't buy more house than you need.

Renovate rather than build.

Don't purchase prepared foods.

Go for quality, not quantity.

Use energy-efficient appliances.

Recycle clothing, furniture, and other goods within your community.

Engage in socially responsible investing.

Use public transportation.

habit of creating a financial margin of safety will feed off, reinforce, and draw energy from each other.

People will differ in how much sustainability enters into their thinking and affects their everyday lives. Most people today make an effort to recycle and upgrade to more energy-efficient household appliances. Many of us try to buy local, organically grown food. Some people have ditched a car, and many more are downsizing to fuel-efficient cars, including hybrids. *Green* is Corporate America's favorite buzzword. Yes, there's green hype and marketing deception, so-called green wash. Still, companies are coming out with increasingly eco-friendly products, and the trend will only gather strength with time. Even during the Great Recession sales of socially and environmentally conscious products and services stayed strong.

Of course, people who agree on the need for creating a better balance between consumption and conservation can vehemently disagree on public-policy initiatives to address global warming and promote alternative energy. But those disagreements shouldn't mask how widespread is the embrace of the values of sustainability.

Values Matter

We don't make financial choices in a vacuum. Savings isn't just money. It's a tool that's critical for creating the kind of life we want to lead. Both a Cadillac Escalade and a Toyota Prius will get us to work and the kids to after-school activities. Yet the former is a nearly fifty-seven-hundred-pound behemoth with a fuel economy of fourteen miles per gallon. The Prius is a small vehicle that gets about fifty miles a gallon. The latter is better for your bank account. It is also a far more environmentally friendly car. Similarly, we can invest savings in tobacco stocks or in solar-power companies. Both investments offer the prospect of a return. But the values they express are different. "Investors who abhor smoking or environmental degradation are regularly told by financial advisers that they should choose stocks that yield the highest returns, including stocks of companies that produce tobacco or pollute the environment, and then donate their profits to campaigns for the causes they support," wrote Meir Statman, finance professor at Santa Clara University, in an article for *Fortune*. "But it is fundamentally flawed. In fact, it's akin to suggesting to an Orthodox Jew that he forgo kosher food for cheaper nonkosher food and donate the savings to his synagogue."

The frugal are conscious consumers that try to be mindful of the ecological and social effect of their purchases and activities. Frugality isn't cheapness. You can be frugal and a generous host. Cheapness doesn't take the needs and feelings of your guests into account. The frugal approach seeks out quality, not quantity. "Cheapskates aim to buy as much as they can for as little as possible, not caring much for the quality or environmental or ethical virtues of the items they're consuming," writes Farhad Manjoo, technology columnist for the online magazine *Slate*. "To be frugal, on the other hand, is to consider the full ramifications of every purchase."

Here's an example of being frugal. My bike got stolen a few years ago because I forgot to lock it. I went to a local bike shop in the Twin Cities to replace it. A woman was shopping for a bike at the same time, but she was in the market for a much more expensive bike than me, something in the $2,000 range. Yet she was getting rid of her car. She was going to use the bike to commute to work to reduce her carbon footprint. She'd take the bus when Minnesota's frigid winters made biking too uncomfortable. So, while she seemed to be spending a hefty sum she was really saving a lot of money after taking into account no more gas station visits, no car maintenance costs, and no car insurance premiums. Why not buy a cool-looking high-tech bike that would make her commute enjoyable. It was a frugal purchase.

When researching the themes of this book I realized that I grew up in a frugal and green household. The former was deliberate. The latter wasn't. It was a consequence of being mindful of spending. We wore heavy sweaters during the winter, since my parents ran the thermostat low to keep down the heating bill. My mother's mom was a seamstress and she made us pajamas every year. My mom bought furniture at thrift stores and had it restored. We wore a lot of hand-me-downs. We didn't eat fast food or frozen dinners (much to our dismay). But food from a farmers market? Whenever possible, yes. Leftovers? You bet. My mom never turned on the dryer in the various homes we lived in. She always preferred a clothesline. When we went on family vacations it was during the off-season when prices were low. My dad's job was to unplug the appliances at night before going to bed. However, my parents were never cheap with us on the things that matter, like health and education. Indeed, all four of their children got good college educations and graduated with no student loans. (Once we were out of the house and on our own they splurged, but off current income and accumulated savings, not borrowed money.)

Frugality is sustainable. Cheapness isn't. The Latin derivation of the word *frugal* is *frugalis*, which means "virtuous, thrifty," according to the *American Heritage Dictionary*. The Latin base for *frugalis* is *frux* and *frug*, words for "fruit" and "virtue." I like the idea that frugality signals virtue bearing fruit through our savings, spending, and giving decisions.

A Word on Perspective

You won't find many financial calculations in these pages. No Greek symbols. No complex equations. You also won't find any action plan for getting rich fast. I don't believe anyone who says he has a surefire quick moneymaking formula, from Donald Trump to Robert Kiyosaki. Paying attention to the siren song of wealth with no money down is a certain path toward wasted time and lost money. I'm not a survivalist, either, fearful that tomorrow will be awful and the day after that even worse. I don't understand putting every scrap of savings into gold and stockpiling food waiting for economic Armageddon. That's no way to live. The fifteenth-century French poet Charles d'Orléans wisely wrote, "It's very well to be thrifty, but don't amass a hoard of regrets." I'm my father's son, neither Pollyanna nor Grinch.

My goal is to have a conversation about managing money and sustainability. To that end, I'll put our current money concerns into a larger economic and historical setting. How did we end up borrowing so much? Why do I believe the New Frugality has staying power this time around when earlier vows to be thrifty were swiftly forgotten once the good times returned? What does the New Frugality mean for dealing with our major financial challenges, from devising a budget to saving for retirement? I'll offer up money tips throughout the book. I'll also highlight books, Web sites, and other resources for additional research and information.

Perspective matters when dealing with money. With Google, Bing, Wolfram/Alpha, and other search engines, it's relatively easy to find information on money and investing. Web sites that deal with money and personal finance are growing exponentially, and the competition for our attention is constantly improving the products. What is missing is a framework for thinking through the risk and rewards of your personal-finance choices as you try to lead a good life. Our financial experience is reminiscent of these haunting lines by T. S. Eliot: "Where is the wisdom we have lost in knowledge? Where is the knowledge we have lost in information?" What I want to do is offer up a coherent point of view for dealing with the money side of everyday life. I'll emphasize risk, a margin of safety, simplicity, and sustainability. You probably won't agree with all my points of emphasis or shades of argument during our conversation about the New Frugality. That's fine, especially if the disagreements help you figure out what will work better for you. After all, that's what really matters.

CHAPTER 2

The Great Transformation

I have no doubt that some of you who read this book ... are
trying to get out of debt, a very ancient slough.

—Henry David Thoreau

LONG AGO I LEARNED THAT WALL STREET veterans are fond of scoffing at anyone who dares suggest America is entering a "new era." Financiers will shake their head with world-weary eyes and quote the pioneering mutual-fund investor Sir John Templeton: "The four most expensive words in the English language are 'this time it's different.'"

There's hard-earned insight behind this skepticism. Speculative manias throughout history thrived on a belief that new technologies and emerging industries upended the old rules of valuation and behavior. The argument that "this time is different" was used to justify stratospheric prices in everything from the stock market of the Roaring '20s to residential real estate in the 2000s. Eventually, the spell is broken, the bubble bursts, and prices plummet.

Yet every once in a great while the established order of everyday life is truly overthrown and the economy really does change. "Within a few short decades, society rearranges itself—its worldview; its basic values; its social and political structure; its arts; its key institutions," wrote Peter Drucker, the late philosopher of management in *Post-Capitalist Society*.

"Fifty years later, there is a new world. And the people born then cannot even imagine the world in which their grandparents lived and into which their own parents were born."

The signs of a new world are all around us. This time the epicenter of change is the household. The age of excessive consumption supported by consumer borrowing is finished. It took us almost a century of consumer borrowing to get to this point, and as is true in so many aspects of life, we pushed what was essentially a positive development too far. Let's examine the evolution of consumer debt to understand where we are going next. What does this have to do with personal finance? Everything. By understanding the history of debt and consumer spending, we'll gain insight into the rise of the New Frugality—and why *this time is different.*

The American Dream on the Installment Plan

The conventional story is that, long ago, Americans were a thrifty people. The New World was built on a culture of thrift, self-denial, and hard work. Taking on debt was a moral failing. "The second Vice is Lying; the first is Running into Debt," said Benjamin Franklin. But then, the story goes, we lost our way. Americans went on a debt binge in recent decades. We abandoned the values of thrift and industry, whipped out our charge cards, and took out home-equity loans to buy stuff—lots of stuff—from personal computers to iPods to second homes. Debt became a way of life. "A new lifestyle of gratification rather than restraint represented the modern wisdom," writes historian David Tucker in *The Decline of Thrift in America.*

That's a common narrative. There's some truth to it, too. Yet the real story about savings and debt is much more complicated. It's also a fascinating tale.

Americans were avid borrowers even in the early days of the republic. "The equation of debt and decline assumes that once upon a time Americans lived within their means and saved for what they bought," T. J. Jackson Lears, a historian at Rutgers University, declared in a *New York Times* essay. "This is fantasy: there never was a golden age of thrift. Debt has always played an important role in Americans' lives—not merely as a means of instant gratification but also as a strategy for survival and a tool for economic advance." Adds historian Lendol Calder of Augustana College in *Financing the American Dream,* "It is often forgotten, but from Plymouth Rock to the present, American dreams have usually required a lien on the future."

The Pilgrims settled in Plymouth Bay in 1620 with the financial backing from London merchant adventurers. The Pilgrims eventually bought out their investors, paying off the debt in installments. In the eighteenth century, Americans borrowed from family, friends, pawnbrokers, loan sharks, and local savings institutions. In the nineteenth century, the national and state banking industries rapidly expanded. Mark Twain co-authored a novel with Charles Dudley Warner, *The Gilded Age,* and it has this delicious passage on debt, one that captures the borrowing mantra for spectacular debtors from P. T. Barnum to Donald Trump: "Beautiful credit! The foundation of modern society . . . [A] whole nation to instantly recognize point and meaning in the familiar newspaper anecdote, which puts into the mouth of a distinguished speculator in lands and mines this remark: 'I wasn't worth a cent two years ago, and now I owe two millions of dollars.'"

Still, much of the business borrowing in the nineteenth century funded the ambitions of America's legendary entrepreneurs. Their boldness and intelligent risk taking created some of the world's most dynamic companies. For instance, debt was critical to the initial fortune earned by the industrial titan Andrew Carnegie. In 1853 Carnegie was seventeen years old, a hustling Scottish immigrant, working as a clerk and telegraph manager for the Pennsylvania Railroad. Carnegie earned $35 a month. A few years later his boss, Thomas Scott, approached his valued employee with an investment opportunity. Problem was, the price of admission was $610. It was a small fortune to Carnegie, living off a clerk's salary. Carnegie borrowed the money from Scott to buy ten shares of Adams Express Company, a competitor to American Express. "The little acorn planted less than a decade previously with Tom Scott's money and ten shares of Adams Express had grown into a mighty oak," according to business historian Richard Tedlow. "The returns from those investments were a staggering $56,100."

Entrepreneurs weren't the only borrowers. Farm families in the nineteenth century routinely ran up debts with local stores. Consumers started buying goods on the installment plan, too. Historians trace the first example of installment credit in America—the classic formula of buy now, pay later—as far back as 1807, to the furniture store Cowperthwaite & Sons. Other furniture stores soon copied the practice.

The really big shift in consumer borrowing came in the early twentieth century with the automobile. Cars were expensive, out of reach for most family budgets. The solution: Buy now, pay later. The pioneer was the financing arm of General Motors, the General Motors Acceptance Corp. By the late 1920s, 65 to 70 percent of cars were bought on credit, according to Martha Olney, economist at the University of California, Berkeley. All sorts of household items were bought on credit, too. "It was hardly an exaggeration to say that the American standard of living was bought on the installment plan," quipped the historian Daniel Boorstin.

Of course, America's eagerness to embrace consumer debt horrified advocates of self-restraint. The sociologists Robert and Helen Lynd were appalled. In the 1920s, the scholars investigated changing social beliefs in a "typical" American city. They settled on Muncie, Indiana. Their results were published in 1929 as *Middletown: A Study in Modern American Culture*. Muncie residents thought of themselves as thrifty savers. But the Lynds saw them differently. "Middletown lives by a credit economy that is available in some form to nearly every family in the community," they wrote. "The rise and spread of the dollar-down-and-so-much-per plan extends credit for virtually everything—homes, $200 over-stuffed living-room suites, electric washing machines, automobiles, fur coats, diamond rings to persons of whom frequently little is known as to their intention or ability to pay."

The two sociologists believed that consumer credit undermined the community's financial and cultural health. Yet when Robert Lynd returned to Muncie during the Great Depression, he learned something remarkable: Few borrowers defaulted on their debts. They did cut back on their spending. "People give up everything in the world but their car," Muncie residents told him again and again.

Muncie was indeed typical. The default rate on auto loans in the late 1920s was around three for every one hundred cars sold on installment, according to Calder. Yet during the darkest years of the depression that figure rose to only five out of one hundred. "Households did not default en masse," writes economist Olney, in the article "Spendthrift or Sophisticate Borrower?" "The sales finance industry was 'a safer investment in 1933 than cash in banks.'"

The consumer borrowing experience of the Great Depression taught bankers that households were an excellent risk. Bankers put that knowledge to good use in the postwar era.

It's a Wonderful Life

Lending is an act of trust. The lender has to believe that the debtor will repay the loan. Borrowing is a strong statement of optimism. The

 Frank Capra's 1946 movie *It's a Wonderful Life* is a charming tale that brings alive a big question: What makes life worth living? The movie is also a story about borrowing. One of the most memorable scenes about money in any movie is an exchange between the banker Mr. Potter and George Bailey (played by Jimmy Stewart). Peter Bailey, George Bailey's father and the founder of Bailey Brothers Building & Loan, had died. Mr. Potter is a coldhearted, avaricious banker. Mr. Potter and George Bailey have a tense exchange at a Building & Loan board meeting:

POTTER: You see, if you shoot pool with some employee here, you can come and borrow money. What does that get us? A discontented, lazy rabble instead of a thrifty working class. And all because a few starry-eyed dreamers like Peter Bailey stir them up and fill their heads with a lot of impossible ideas . . .

GEORGE: . . . But he did help a few people get out of your slums, Mr. Potter. And what's wrong with that? Doesn't it make them better citizens? Doesn't it make them better customers? You, you said that, what'd you say just a minute ago, they had to wait and save their money before they even thought of a decent home.

Wait! Wait for what? Until their children grow up and leave them? . . . Do you know how long it takes a working man to save five thousand dollars? Just remember this, Mr. Potter, that this rabble you're talking about, they do most of the working and paying and living and dying in this community.

Well, is it too much to have them work and pay and live and die in a couple of decent rooms and a bath?

No, it's not too much to ask. The working people in the movie, many of them immigrants, borrowed to have a place to call their own.

borrower has faith that the future will be good enough for him or her to repay the debt. The American Dream is essentially a story of optimism. Immigrants come here to make a better life for themselves and their children. Entrepreneurs believe customers will flock to their new business. Homeowners borrow enormous sums to buy a house convinced that tomorrow will be better than today.

My dad was one of those optimistic borrowers when he bought his first home in Levittown, America's most famous postwar suburb. Between

1947 and 1951 the developer William Levitt adapted factory-inspired assembly-line techniques to construct more than seventeen thousand homes in Nassau County, Long Island. Levittown became the prototypical suburb reviled in books such as *Revolutionary Road* and *Catcher in the Rye*. But World War II veterans and their families who bought these affordable homes loved Levittown and similar developments. "To these people, the new suburbs were an affordable paradise," says historian John Steele Gordon in *An Empire of Wealth: The Epic History of American Economic Power.*

That's how my parents felt. They moved to Levittown in 1949. After World War II, my dad was attached to Kings Point, the Merchant Marine Academy on Long Island. My parents rented the top floor of a nearby mansion. The bathroom ceiling was so low my father had to kneel to shave. Their next home, in Springfield Gardens, Queens, was not much better. Dad could shave standing up. But the walls of the apartment were so thin my mom says you could hear everything that went on next door, above and below.

Like many men after the war, my father attended night school. He went to Columbia University, and there he saw a brochure for Levittown. My parents purchased a two-bedroom Cape Cod–style house. The home had radiant heat, a refrigerator, and a washer. The price of homeownership: $7,990. They put $90 down, and the monthly mortgage, insurance, and tax payment totaled $58. Translated into current dollars, they bought a $72,000 home with $815 down. They loved their new home.

My grandfather was furious at my father for buying a home. He had worked as the head bookkeeper at Anaconda Copper, the giant mining company in New York. During the Great Depression, he saw almost all of the thirty employees in his department laid off.

He, too, had borrowed to buy a home, taking out an interest-only mortgage in the 1920s. As in the 2000s housing bubble, borrowers expected to refinance their interest-only mortgages after a few years as housing values rose. It worked out okay during the '20s.

Of course, when the Depression struck, prices fell and many homeowners couldn't refinance. The bank foreclosed on my grandfather. His family crowded into a two-bedroom rental apartment in Yonkers, some-times as many as seven people. The torture of watching his colleagues lose their jobs one or two at a time and then losing his home made my grandfather deeply fearful of debt. He shunned it. He never owned a home again, and he truly believed my father was ruining his life and squander-ing his family's future by taking out a mortgage. Yet my parents were optimistic. They borrowed. It paid off for them and millions of other Americans in the postwar era.

President Franklin D. Roosevelt backed that optimism with the GI Bill of Rights. It was a sweeping program of benefits, including government-backed home loans. Thirty-year mortgages became industry standard be-cause of the GI Bill. FDR made it possible for millions of Americans to buy a home and to start building up equity. Put somewhat differently, the GI Bill introduced a whole generation to the potential benefits of long-term debt. The radio documentary producer Stephen Smith rightly calls FDR "the most influential mortgage broker of the 20th century."

When Jerry Ulrich returned to Minnesota from the U.S. Navy after the war, he and his wife Gertrude wanted to buy a house in the budding Min-neapolis suburb of Richfield. They had little money. But they got a home because the federal government backed their mortgage. The GI Bill also paid for Jerry's dental school and it provided a low-interest business loan so Jerry could set up a practice. Gertrude Ulrich and her husband paid their bills on schedule, raised six children, and sent them all to college. Gertrude says it's all because the government made it possible for a young sailor and his wife to borrow some money, and to work their way into the middle class.

It's fair to say that the GI Bill helped build the modern American sub-urb. And suburbia meant shopping malls, interstate highways and the baby boom. With more credit available, Americans bought more con-sumer goods like cars, refrigerators, and televisions.

The Democratization of Credit

It's striking that as early as 1954 the American historian David M. Potter could write, "The compilation of statistics might be extended endlessly, but it would only prove repetitively that in every aspect of material plenty America possesses unprecedented riches and that these are very widely distributed among one hundred and fifty million American people. If few can cite the figures, everyone knows that we have, per capita, more automobiles, more telephones, more radios, more vacuum cleaners, more electric lights, more bathtubs, more supermarkets and movie palaces and hospitals, than any other nation." Fact is, most of those goods were bought on the installment plan. The postwar years marked the high point of American prosperity.

The year 1958 was a watershed in the history of consumer credit. BankAmerica launched a general-purpose credit card in Fresno, California, with three hundred retailers and nearly sixty thousand cardholders. By the end of the following year those numbers had swelled to twenty-five thousand merchants and nearly two million cardholders. That experiment eventually led to the credit cards we're familiar with today, such as Visa and MasterCard. A majority of American households have at least one credit card, and government statisticians calculate that some 1.5 billion credit cards are in use in the United States.

Another consumer-debt milestone was the inflationary spiral of the 1970s. Inflation erodes the value of a dollar. By definition, inflation is a decline in the purchasing power of money, and the higher the rate of inflation the steeper the drop. The consumer price index—the main measure of changes in the overall price level—soared into double-digit territory in the seventies. Inflation is devastating for savers, but it is the borrower's friend. After all, you're paying off yesterday's loan with dollars that are worth less today. "My parents could tell me till I'm blue in the face debt is bad, debt is bad, debt is bad," says *New York Times* columnist Joseph Nocera. "But my experience told me debt is good."

The "democratization of credit" marched on even after inflation rates subsided. The credit card, the home mortgage, the student loan, the auto

Journalist William H. Whyte Jr. chronicled the evolution of business culture and suburban living in a remarkable series of articles for *Fortune* in the 1950s. He captured the borrowing ethos of the new suburban middle class in a 1956 article, "Budgetism: Opiate of the Middle Class": "They save little not because they cannot save—people have never been more prosperous. They save little because they do not really believe in saving . . . the people who are most responsible for the dangerous increase in mortgage and short-term debt are younger couples in the $5,000-to-$7,500 bracket. Sober suburbia is their habitat . . . And they are the true prodigals."

Whyte details a typical young middle-class suburban-family budget. Ed Doe is a twenty-nine-year-old accountant. He's married to Mary and earns $6,000 a year. They have two children.

Whyte takes a look at Ed's paycheck. He nets $416.34 on his $500 paycheck after automatic deductions. When Ed writes the bills, he pays out $80 for the mortgage, $54 for a car loan, $21 on a life insurance premium, $14.75 for their furniture loan, $18.30 on a medical bill, $15 on a revolving credit to a department store, $6.18 to the telephone company, and $20 to the utility company. That leaves them with about $190. Ed sets aside $100 or so in the checking account for food, and $39 to $45 goes toward church, gas, car maintenance, and the newspaper boy. They have about $45 left. "This must provide for clothing, entertainment, drugstore purchases, cleaning, laundry, a part-time cleaning woman once a week, baby sitters, cigarettes—not to mention any savings," writes Whyte. "There will not, of course, be enough money. But no matter; the deficit can easily be taken care of by another loan. Ed and Mary are glad they live so conservatively." Sound familiar?

loan, and other types of consumer credit were widespread tools for getting ahead. Loans once limited to the well-heeled were gradually offered to middle-income and then lower-income households. Women could get credit on their own rather than through their husbands. Minority neighborhoods were no longer redlined. Banks even solicited business from illegal immigrants. Credit was everywhere.

The Wages of Debt

That's the positive side of the consumer-credit narrative. It's also true that throughout our history people took on too much debt. Michael Boyle was a salaried employee in St. Paul, Minnesota, in the late 1880s. An Irish American, he had improved his standard of living from a dry goods day laborer to a buyer and seller of ginghams, prints, and jeans over the previous decade, according to the social historian Jocelyn Wills of Brooklyn College. Yet on the eve of his thirty-first birthday, a miserable Boyle wrote in his diary, "I am powerless because I am in debt and clearly my first duty is to get out of that condition. This is the harvest one reaps when one sows in extravagance and dissipation."

I imagine Boyle would have agreed with the definition of debt penned by the nineteenth-century journalist Ambrose Bierce: "Debt, n. An ingenious substitute for the chain and whip of the slave-driver."

The tragedy of William Rodriquez briefly gained notoriety in 1960. He was a twenty-three-year-old Puerto Rican living in Chicago with his wife and their four children. He owed about $700, most of it for furniture, clothing, a secondhand television set, and a religious medal he'd bought for his mother. His wages had been garnisheed three times before, and a lender was threatening garnishment again. Rodriquez killed himself on a cold February evening. The coroner's verdict: "Suicide while temporarily insane due to pressure from creditors."

The merchants of debt promote the convenience of credit but hide the true costs. Through various methods they hike rates and fees on consumers. When regulators crack down on certain practices, ingenious new ones are developed. "It is the life of quiet desperation, the ceaseless tension, the fear of ultimate impoverishment that haunt so many, who because of modest means find themselves chained to the treadmill of never-ending debt," wrote journalist Hillel Black in *Buy Now, Pay Later*, a 1960s exposé about consumer-debt malpractice. Five decades later the same sentence and observation holds for millions of Americans trapped by rapacious payday lenders and unscrupulous credit card issuers.

The Economics of "Budgetism"

Clearly, the consumer-debt revolution that began in the 1920s made it easy for some people to live beyond their means. Yet consumer debt also encouraged something else: middle-class prosperity. And personal spending during the postwar period essentially tracked the overall growth of the economy, adjusted for inflation. Sometimes we'd get ahead of the real economy with our spending and borrowing. We'd back off for a while, especially during recessions. We'd pull back enough so that our spending growth dipped below the economy's growth rate. Then we'd spend more. Throughout the business cycle a majority of borrowers paid their bills on time.

Case in point: the Mall of America, a stunning citadel of consumerism. You can't miss the mall if you drive along Interstate 494 near the Twin Cities' airport. It boasts some 520 stores in a space big enough to hold thirty-two Boeing 747s. The center of the Mall is an indoor amusement park with a roller coaster, a water slide, and other rides. The Mall has movie theaters, an aquarium, adult-education classes, a wedding chapel, and stores—lots of stores.

The Mall was built during the 1990–91 recession. It opened in August 1992. The recession ended the previous spring, but employers were slow to put new workers on their payrolls. A *New York Times* article wondered about the Mall's prospects considering the state of the economy: "Many industry analysts . . . question the sanity of launching a monster mall in the middle of a recession, at a time when studies suggest that

Americans would rather do almost anything with their leisure time other than shop."

Yet four months later a *New York Times* editorial marveled at the megamall on the prairie: "To roam the Mall of America is to mourn those family members and friends who were born to shop but, alas, born too soon to see this monument to credit cards . . . Up and down the escalators they go, in and out of hundreds of stores. Some are laden with packages; others carry only a small bag or two. The empty-handed are rare, perhaps because the urge to make a dent in this vast pile of prodigality is close to overwhelming."

It's easy to make fun of people with a "shop 'till you drop" attitude. Yet critics who highlight the pursuit of immediate gratification by consumers miss an important dynamic: Borrowing on a monthly installment plan for much of the postwar era enforced a kind of economic discipline. Lendol Calder observed, in *Financing the American Dream*, "Far from causing the demise of thrift, consumer credit has actually worked to make most modern credit users at least as disciplined in their finances as the generations that lived before the credit revolution. The fact is, 'easy credit' is really not all that easy. Installment credit imposes on borrowers financial regimens requiring discipline, foresight, and a conscious effort to save income in order to make payments on time."

Calls for greater thrift are appealing during recessions. But is it any wonder that thrift is abandoned when good times reemerge? Our attitude toward thrift and savings has long been a secular variation on a famous remark by Saint Augustine, "Give me chastity and continence, but not yet."

A Stunning Break with Our Money Past

Budgetism broke down in the decade leading up to the Great Recession. The household borrowing boom was unprecedented. To fund the buying of homes, remodeled kitchens, SUVs, personal computers, iPods, college tuitions, vacations, and other goods and services, Americans borrowed so much that household debt hit a record 131 percent of annual dispos-able income in early 2008: We owed a third more than we were taking home each year after taxes. The household debt ratio was 90 percent a decade earlier and less than 80 percent the decade before that. Little wonder the personal savings rate—the share of income left after our spending—went from the 8 percent range in the mid-1980s to almost zero during the height of the housing bubble.

The epicenter of the borrowing mania was housing. The initial stages of the housing market's gains were mostly driven by improving funda-mentals. Mortgage rates in the early 2000s were almost as low as in the 1950s. The after-tax cost of mortgage payments absorbed 18.5 percent of household income in 2001, down considerably from 22.5 percent in 1990. Competition in the home-mortgage market had lowered fees and loosened down-payment requirements. The lure of owning a home in-creased after some $8 trillion in stock market wealth vaporized during the dot-com bust and the trauma of 9/11. A four-bedroom, center-hall colonial, a one-bedroom condo with a brick wall, a town house nestled along a mountain ridge, and even a mobile home blocks from the ocean are made of solid materials. A common remark at the time was, if you owned stock, you had nothing of value when it went down. If the price of a house fell, you still had a place to call your own. Everyone wanted to talk about real estate. I remember in the years between 2004 and 2006 taking calls from listeners berating me for my cautious advice on home-ownership. Real estate prices kept spiraling higher, and buyers danger-ously stretched their finances to buy. Owners treated their home equity like an ATM.

The borrowing binge went beyond housing. People bought every-thing from aged balsamic vinegars to Sub-Zero refrigerators on credit. The average cost of a wedding soared to nearly $30,000. Students and their families borrowed record sums to pay for college. Car loans reached an average of nearly $31,000, up almost 40 percent over the past de-cade. Almost half of all car loans were six years or longer, a sure way to owe more than the car is worth. The flush times couldn't last, and didn't.

The largest consumer-borrowing boom in U.S. history went spectacularly bust starting in 2007. The canary in the debt coal mine was the collapse of the subprime mortgage market. But consumer-credit problems quickly rippled throughout the credit economy. The worst financial crisis since the 1930s hit the housing market hard. Companies shoved millions of workers out the door. The bust unveiled breathtaking instances of greed by the heads of financial institutions. At Washington Mutual, CEO Kerry Killinger pocketed more than $88 million in the years leading up to one of the biggest banking failures in history. The downturn uncovered monumental frauds, such as the multibillion-dollar Ponzi scheme run by Bernard Madoff. The Federal Reserve, the U.S. Treasury, and the Federal Deposit Insurance Corporation (FDIC) took unprecedented actions to prevent the recession from plunging into something far worse. "I never thought I would live to see a recurrence of things I did see up close during the Great Depression," says Paul Samuelson, the Nobel laureate in economics.

Talking to a legendary economist about the financial crisis and the prospects for another depression is one way to measure the extraordinary time we went through. A far more personal marker is to pick up the phone and have your eighty-three-year-old mother ask you, in all seriousness, "Are we going into another Great Depression?"

"No, I don't think so," I said. I quickly ran through my reasons. I was confident that Federal Reserve Board chairman Ben Bernanke, a scholar of the Great Depression, would do whatever it would take to prevent a reprise of the 1930s. The bank bailouts engineered by U.S. Treasury Secretary Henry Paulson and his successor, Tim Geithner, may have been flawed, but they were critical for shoring up the system.

"Well, I hope you're right," she said. "But you didn't think it would get this bad either."

BUSTED. LATER, Mom assured me that I could always move back in with her. Several of her friends from school had had to move back in with their parents in the thirties. She meant it, and it was a touching moment, a sign of the perilous times we were in. Thankfully, a depression was averted.

I won't have to move in with Mom. And Americans won't go back to borrowing as usual.

Stagnant Incomes, Loopy Lenders

Plenty of culprits are to blame for the financial crisis, but I want to highlight the ominous combination of stagnant incomes and lender profligacy. These two factors help account for the staying power of the New Frugality.

Remember, borrowers are optimistic. When the economy left the 2001 recession behind, people started borrowing again in anticipation of earning better incomes. It had happened before. From the 1969 business cycle peak to the 1979 peak, household income grew by 4.5 percent after adjusting for inflation, according to economist Jared Bernstein. The comparable figure for 1979 to 1989 was 6.5 percent, and from 1989 to 2000, 8.3 percent. Problem is, from 2000 to 2007 real household income fell by 0.6 percent, he calculates. The income gains households reasonably anticipated didn't happen.

Bernstein dissected the household income numbers even further. He calculated that the real median income of working-age households—those headed by someone less than sixty-five—rose by some 10 percent or $5,200 between 1989 and 2000. The experience of working-age households in the subsequent business cycle was dismayingly different. He figures that the income of working-age households fell $2,000 between 2000 and 2007, from about $58,500 to $56,500. Households were forced to pay for rising energy, food, and health insurance costs on a shrunken income. For instance, an estimated 116 million people, or two-thirds of working-age adults, were either uninsured for a time, faced steep out-of-pocket medical costs relative to their incomes, had difficulties paying their medical bills, or didn't get the care they needed because of cost in 2007, according to a Commonwealth Fund Biennial Health Insurance

Survey. Oil prices, which had been as low as $20 a barrel in 2001, reached $100 in late 2007 and peaked at $145 a barrel in July 2008.

Optimists who thought incomes would grow turned out to be wrong, deeply wrong.

Lenders love to promote themselves as sober-minded guardians of credit. The lending industry wraps itself in the high-minded mantle of meeting the aspirations and desires of ordinary Americans through the steady march toward a "democratization of credit." What many lenders actually did in the 2000s is abandon reason and ethics. Jamie Dimon, chief executive officer of JPMorgan Chase, squarely puts the blame on lenders for allowing consumers to borrow far too much. "We gave them the weapons of mass destruction to borrow too much," said Dimon at a global economic forum. "I don't blame them. I blame the CEOs."

In the background of the lending boom was one of the most significant and heartening transformations in history: globalization. In essence, that means the closer integration of India, China, Vietnam, and other emerging markets into the rest of the world economy. One result was a dramatic increase in global savings, which, in turn, helped drive down interest rates. John Maynard Keynes once quoted Walter Bagehot, the legendary nineteenth-century editor of the *Economist*, that "John Bull can stand many things, but he cannot stand 2 per cent." In search of higher yields, British investors were eager to invest huge sums in railroads and other risky but potentially lucrative ventures in nineteenth-century America.

The same desire for high-yield debt dominated the action in the global capital markets of the 2000s. Financiers found plenty of eager buyers for riskier securities that paid significantly better rates than low-yielding U.S. government bonds. Lenders learned that Wall Street's appetite for consumer loans was insatiable and meeting the demand profitable. Wall Street's math whizzes became increasingly creative at making securities from home mortgages, student loans, auto loans, and credit cards. Financial alchemists transformed risky loans into triple-A-rated securities.

Financiers were making so much money that no one wanted to stop. Why take away the punch bowl when the party's going strong? Predatory

lenders trolled through poor neighborhoods taking advantage of unso-
phisticated borrowers. Banks did business with speculators eager to own
and flip several homes. Don't want to report your income? We got a loan
for you—at a higher interest rate, of course. Can't put any money down
for that home? How about an interest-only mortgage that resets at a
higher interest rate in a couple of years? Your daughter is heading off to
college and you're carrying too much in credit card debt? Consolidate all
your debts into a home-equity loan. You're a student without an income?
Here's a credit card.

It was open season for shoveling all kinds of credit at people. That is,
until the borrowing boom went bust.

This Time Is Different

Memories linger. We remember dramatic economic events long after the
underlying environment has changed. Those memories shape our financial behavior. However, our memories are selective and tend to focus on
the downside. "The memory bank we carried forward from the 1920s
was filled with the anguish of the Great Crash and then the Great Depression, not the revolutionary technological innovations of the automobile, electric power, and the radio," wrote financier Peter Bernstein. The
generation that lived through the Great Depression steered clear of equities in the 1950s even though stock market values were incredibly attractive, he added. The generation that lived through the Age of Inflation
learned it was smart to borrow. They continued to borrow big even after
inflation was tamed. The Great Recession has taught all of us that it's financially dangerous to carry too much debt. It's a lesson that will shape
our finances for years. Bankers and regulators have memories, too. The
financial system was bailed out by the federal government, and lenders
wrote off billions and billions of dollars in bad debts. Bankers are demanding more conservative financing from potential borrowers, and regulators are frowning at any signs of loose lending practices.

The Great Recession vividly demonstrated how vulnerable indebted

Americans are to a setback. Jobs and incomes are less secure than ever with restructurings, downsizings, reengineering, rightsizing—pick your favorite euphemism—a routine part of management's strategic toolkit. Management during the Great Recession controlled costs by adopting pay freezes, furloughs, and pay cuts. Employers reduced their financial support of worker pensions, too. The typical employer matches 3 percent to 5 percent of employee contributions into a 401(k) plan, but many companies suspended their matching program during the Great Recession. Cost-cutting initiatives like these will become routine, just as layoffs did following the severe recession of the early 1980s. "My view is that Americans, from the working poor to the reasonably rich, are in danger of taking steep financial falls from which they have a terrible time recovering; that the fraction of Americans facing this danger is on the rise and now constitutes a majority; and that the size of the fall we may take is also growing," writes author Peter Gosselin in *High Wire*, a thoughtful examination of the heightened risk of financial trouble faced by ordinary families. The only way to offset that financial exposure is to save more and borrow less.

That said, saving won't be easy. Incomes will stagnate or grow slowly. Certainly that's been the long-term trend. For example, real median hourly wages have eked out a mere 8 percent gain since 1979. Of course, we own bigger homes, more cars, and more stuff overall than we did in the late 1970s. We're clearly a wealthier society, and not all the gains are from a debt-financed mirage. What happened is that many families boosted their incomes as women entered the workforce. In 1968, 38 percent of married women ages twenty-five to fifty-four with children worked out of the home. That figure is now over 70 percent. Mom and dad also work about 20 percent more hours than in 1968. But the money push from the rise of two-income couples has petered out. No one else can leave home to bring in a wage. It's hard to imagine parents can put in any more hours at work, either. And, sorry, you can't send the kids off to work.

We're going to have to live off what we earn. It will take years for us to make up for the ground lost during the Great Recession. Imagine a pendulum hanging high from a ceiling swinging slowly from side to side in a wide arc. At one end of its swing it's all debt, and at the other ex-treme it's all savings. The pendulum in the 2000s swung way too far in debt's direction. It's now working its way back toward savings. Eventu-ally it will come to rest somewhere in the middle, between all-savings-all-the-time and borrowing-as-much-as-possible. But it takes a long time to pay down that borrowed money. That is what we have to do.

Sustainability Goes Mainstream

Of course, Americans don't like donning economic hairshirts. Words like "frugality" and "savings" seem to signal the embrace of extreme denial and shrunken ambition, with images of sixteenth-century theologian John Calvin and seventeenth-century Puritan minister Cotton Mather stalking American households. But the New Frugality isn't something to glumly embrace. No, it means we're going to live a better way and have fun at the same time.

For one thing, what we're spending our money on is changing. Think back on some of the conversations you had with friends and colleagues during the Great Recession. A common thread of discussion was how much we appreciated experiences with friends and family over buying stuff at the mall and the downtown chain store. The downturn brought that message home. We started putting a high value on a home-cooked meal, an over-fifty hockey game on a frozen pond, and a thirty-mile bike ride with thousands of strangers to raise money for a cause. For many of us, our homes suddenly looked cluttered with too much stuff. Fact is, we have plenty of cars, TVs, shirts and other goods. Nobel laureate Robert Fogel in *The Fourth Great Awakening & The Future of Egalitarianism*, a magisterial economic history of America, notes that "we're approaching saturation in the consumption not only of necessities, but also of goods recently thought to be luxuries or that existed only as dreams of the fu-ture during the first third of the twentieth century."

Despite the trauma of the Great Recession, we're a rich society that can afford nurturing activities that "broaden the mind" and "enrich the soul," says Fogel. He's right. Indeed, the meaning of the American Dream, that famous phrase historian James Truslow Adams came up with during the dark days of the Great Depression, is changing. It has always had something of a dual meaning. The emphasis in recent decades was more on the material side of the idea. Yet the concept has always carried with it the notion of trying to live a good life, engaged in the community, expanding our minds and enriching our souls.

For another, the shift in our outlook and emphasis will get an important impetus from the green revolution. Going green is emotionally satisfying and financially frugal. The personal economics of sustainability will make the transition toward financial conservatism practical and enjoyable. That's right, enjoyable. We'll feel good about ourselves and the actions we take to save more and borrow less while pursuing quality and simplicity. Frugal is the new chic.

Americans have long been concerned about nature and the environment. The list of ecological activists includes President Teddy Roosevelt, John Muir, Rachel Carson, and David Brower. The Environmental Protection Agency was set up in 1970, and despite many bitter fights over green regulations between business and environmentalists, a desire for clean water and air often attracted bipartisan coalitions. Still, the dramatic change over the past two decades has been the science of global climate change. Today, especially because of heightened concern over global warming, the greening of America is apparent in every aspect of our lives. Federal, state, and local governments have all launched various green initiatives. So have schools and colleges. Sustainability is taken seriously by business, too, from Silicon Valley venture capitalists to the CEOs of major multinational corporations. "First of all, we believe sustainability is critical, absolutely key," said John Brock, chairman and chief executive of Coca-Cola Enterprises in an interview at the Wharton School of the University of Pennsylvania. "It's not a niche anymore. It's not just something you kind of do when you're thinking about it. It's something we take seriously, and it has to be done all the time."

Sustainability isn't only a business and government priority. It's something most of us increasingly try to take into account in our actions at home and at work. For those of us trying to save more, an ethos of sustainability provides another screen for being mindful with our money. Being energy conscious at home, buying clothes at yard sales and vintage stores, and similar thrifty actions both save money and reduce our impact on the planet. It's time to simplify.

What's more, embracing sustainability is optimistic. Sure, there are plenty of doom and gloom forecasts about global warming. But at home and in our communities, to be financially frugal and socially sustainable reflects a basic faith that the effort will pay off in a better future for us and our children. Like borrowing in the early postwar years, it's an

---

 Saul Griffith is an inventor, entrepreneur, writer, and MacArthur Fellow. At a talk on the science of climate change and sustainability, he addressed what we can do.

Spend money on services—everything from repairs to education—and not on things

Eat less and more healthy food

Exercise more

Don't just drive less, get rid of the car

Spend more time with family

Spend less time commuting: Live closer to family and friends, work and school

Reduce business travel

Get higher-quality, better-designed products you don't replace, the "Montblanc pen" approach to life

optimistic set of beliefs and behaviors. Unlike borrowing, there's no whiplash of debt payments if we stumble. We just pick up and start the journey again. In conclusion, while Sir John Templeton would roll his eyes at me, I believe this time is different. America is entering a new era. The transformation in what we do with our money and how we manage our finances is profound and long-lasting.

CHAPTER 3

A Margin of Safety

If you have built castles in the air, your work will not be lost; that is where they should be. Now put the foundations under them.

—Henry David Thoreau

To PARAPHRASE THE INVESTING GENIUS Warren Buffett, managing money well over a lifetime doesn't demand a stratospheric IQ, unusual insight, or detailed knowledge of finance. It does take a "sound intellectual framework for making decisions and the ability to keep emotions from corroding that framework." Let's focus on the building blocks of a sensible money-management and lifestyle framework for the New Frugality.

You Can't Get Rid of Uncertainty

A key concept is that we don't know the future. Okay, it's such an obvious point, why make it? Well, the older you get, the more you appreciate the insight (despite rising dismay at graying hair and a sagging middle). Peter Bernstein, the late dean of finance economists and a philosopher of risk, liked to say that we can't pierce the fog of the future. It's in the nature of the beast.

When Western Union was offered the chance to buy Alexander Graham Bell's 1876 telephone patent for $100,000, management declined because the telephone had "too many shortcomings to be seriously considered as a means of communication." Instead, Western Union offered to withdraw from the telephone business in return for Bell's promise not to compete with it in the telegraph business. In the 1940s, Thomas Watson Sr., president of IBM, then one of the world's leading adding-machine companies, confidently predicted, "There is a market for maybe five computers." Oops.

Many investors are intrigued by the possibility of making money buying stocks in frontier market economies, such as China and India. The risks are obvious, but the potential rewards if you're right are huge. Which countries do you think will enjoy political stability and the rule of law two decades from now, and which ones will have descended into chaos? China? Malaysia? Brazil? Venezuela? "You have a pretty good idea of what is going to happen a minute from now, the rest of today, tomorrow, and possibly the rest of the week," said Bernstein. "As the time horizon expands, uncertainty increases because the range of possible outcomes widens as we look further and further into the future."

As Yogi Berra put it, "It's tough to make predictions, especially about the future."

History is full of shocks and surprises, unexpected twists and turns, both on the downside and the upside. You've probably heard that over the past two centuries the U.S. stock market has sported an average annual return of about 7 percent, adjusted for inflation. Yet on average Lake Erie never freezes. Even a casual glance at history shows investors struggling to cope with bear markets and bull markets, cataclysms such as World War I, World War II, September 11, and the Great Recession. The surprises aren't all negative. We've also lived through radical new technologies that have changed the way we live and work, such as the railroads, personal computers, and the Internet. We have to manage our money through the tumult. We can't eliminate the uncertainty.

Don't Pull an Avery

What you don't want to do is act like Avery. As in Sewell Avery. He went into a bunker.

The retailing giant Montgomery Ward was losing money during the Great Depression. The investment bank J. P. Morgan (which had a stake in Ward) convinced Avery, a highly successful CEO, to run Ward and stem the flood of red ink in 1931. Avery succeeded. According to *Time,* in three years he turned a $9 million loss into a $9 million profit. Avery ruled with an iron hand, once remarking, "If anybody ventures to differ with me, of course, I throw them out of the window."

Avery famously hated President Franklin Roosevelt and the New Deal. When Roosevelt in 1944 ordered the federal government to seize Ward's Chicago plant for the war effort, Avery refused to cooperate. A remarkable photo captured him being carried out of Ward's Chicago headquarters by two soldiers who "picked 170-lb. Sewell Avery up by his arms and thighs, carried him to the elevator," wrote *Time.* "Mr. Avery refused to walk in; the soldiers picked him up again. In the elevator Sewell Avery said: 'I'll be glad when this is over.' On the main floor he again refused to budge. The soldiers hoisted him up, carried him past a handful of startled clerks in the lobby, and down the main steps. His grey hair unruffled, his blue suit coat buttoned, his hands folded benignly across his stomach, his eyes half-closed, Avery looked every inch an Oriental potentate being borne by slaves . . . Put down on the sidewalk, Sewell Avery bowed slightly to his carriers, walked across the Chicago, Milwaukee, St. Paul & Pacific Railroad tracks to a waiting limousine."

Avery was convinced another Great Depression would follow World War II. He got Ward ready for the inevitable collapse. He hoarded cash, refused to spend money on expansion, and got rid of costly talent. The result of his bunker mentality was that Avery missed the biggest consumer-spending boom in history—the post–World War II golden era. "Most companies soon responded, including Montgomery Ward's archrival, Sears, Roebuck. But Avery, now in his seventies, had become a sort of reverse Herbert Hoover, insisting that depression was just around the corner," writes .

historian John Steele Gordon in *American Heritage* magazine. "The results were disastrous. Sears's sales doubled in the ten years following the war, while Montgomery Ward's shrank 10 percent." The company never really recovered and closed its stores in 2001.

Don't Be like Durant

You also don't want to pretend uncertainty doesn't exist. Starry-eyed optimism finally undid William "Billy" Crapo Durant. He's not well remembered today, but Durant was an extraordinary character. He founded General Motors, creating the American automobile industry along with Henry Ford.

Durant was a charming man of imperial ambitions. A wealthy buggy manufacturer, he took over Buick Motor Co., a defunct carmaker with one factory, in 1904. Four years later he created General Motors. He wasn't a manager, however. He liked to cut deals, not focus on administrative and organizational tasks. Durant was forced out of GM in 1910. The next year he formed Chevrolet and managed to regain control of GM in 1915. Durant went on an empire-building spree, snapping up some thirty companies, according to Martin Fridson in *It Was a Very Good Year*. By 1919, Durant had cobbled together the nation's fifth-largest industrial empire. Yet he was once again forced out, this time during the sharp recession of 1920. The company was foundering through mismanagement. The board of directors also learned that Durant had secretly been trying to prop up the company's stock price. He took on some $38 million in personal debt manipulating GM's stock. The House of Morgan, along with the wealthy Du Pont family, engineered a bailout of GM. Durant lost a fortune and was pushed out of the company. He quickly established another automaker.

But Durant had found a far better playground for his speculative verve. He transferred his passion and optimism to Wall Street. He loved betting on stocks. Durant bought equities on the belief they would go up and up (and he participated in various manipulations common among plungers at the time to boost stock prices just in case). His optimism paid off fabulously during the Roaring '20s. But he was wiped out during the Great Depression. In 1936 he filed for bankruptcy. What did he have left? According to his bankruptcy filing, he owed $814,000 and all he owned were the clothes on his back, worth $250. Later on he ran a bowling alley in Flint, Michigan. He died in New York in 1947, poor and largely forgotten.

Be like Aristotle

Instead of acting like Avery or Durant, why not emulate Aristotle, the Greek philosopher. He's my favorite personal financial planner. Intellectual historians often credit him with developing the idea of the good life, an examined life of meaning and purpose in contrast to merely getting by and gratifying immediate desires. Aristotle lived in the fourth century B.C., and his thoughts were gathered together in the *Nicomachean Ethics*. In his lectures he expounds on his most famous idea: the golden mean. It's that desirable although elusive middle between two extremes. The mean "lies between excess and deficiency," says Aristotle. The *Stanford Encyclopedia of Philosophy* illustrates the concept with this example: "The courageous person, for example, judges that some dangers are worth facing and others not, and experiences fear to a degree that is appropriate to his circumstances. He lies between the coward, who flees every danger and experiences excessive fear, and the rash person, who judges every danger worth facing and experiences little or no fear." It's how I believe my dad led his life.

The practical financial application of the golden mean is better known as a *margin of safety*. It's the bedrock idea of personal finance for all seasons and at all ages, from a high school graduate trying to decide between a public university and a private college, to an aging worker wrestling with how much money to put into fixed-income securities and how much into equities. A margin-of-safety perspective helps steer you between the extremes of an Avery and a Durant, between the Scylla of fear and

Charybdis of greed. It helps us understand the financial consequences of being wrong while being ready to take advantage of opportunities. A margin of safety is the most valuable concept for individuals and families managing their money.

What is the margin of safety in practice? A classic example is to have an emergency savings fund that would pay for your household's expenses for up to a year. That's a margin of safety against a layoff. The same cash cushion gives you the financial freedom to switch jobs. Buying life insurance to protect your family in case you unexpectedly die is another time-honored margin-of-safety tactic. When it comes to retirement savings, the basic money question you should ask yourself is not "How much money will I make on my investments?" The real question is "How much can I afford to lose?" You then lock in a standard of living for your old age with a conservative investment strategy. You don't want to be seventy years old with a portfolio that has lost half its value. The financial specifics of everyone's margin of safety can differ, but the basic perspective holds.

Sustainability is also a margin-of-safety perspective in a big and a small way. The science of global warming is convincing that the planet is in danger, for example. The longer we wait, the worse it could get. Of course, a great deal of uncertainty surrounds global warming's possible impact on the planet. Policies to aggressively address greenhouse emissions are the equivalent of taking out a planetary margin of safety. At a more personal level, incorporating sustainability habits into our everyday money decisions creates a margin of safety almost by definition. Rock rebel Janis Joplin in the 1960s sarcastically sang, "Oh, Lord, won't you buy me a Mercedes-Benz? My friends all drive Porsches. I must make amends." Well, consuming with a conscience moves us away from taking out loans for expensive stuff we don't really need or using credit cards to buy items on a whim. Being wary of debt removes a major source of everyday emotional stress and financial pressure.

There's an added, underappreciated benefit of a sustainable sensibility: Control. I don't know where the stock market will be a decade from now, and neither do you. Inflation could take off or remain dormant.

But I can control where I spend my money. I can support certain businesses and causes with my dollars. I can recycle the stuff I no longer want and get it to people who need it more. I also know that experiences with family and friends are far more valuable than possessions, and I can take advantage of that insight every day. "If we do not serve what coheres and endures, we serve what disintegrates and destroys," says Wendell Berry, the farmer and poet.

A margin of safety with a Roth IRA

The Roth IRA is unique, and it's almost the perfect margin-of-safety product. The reason: It's both a long-term retirement savings plan and a parking place for emergency money.

The contributions you make to the Roth are with after-tax dollars. The limit is $5,000. It's $6,000 if you're fifty or over. The contribution limits are adjusted annually for changes in line with inflation starting in 2010. The real kicker is that all the investment gain is free of taxes when you take the money out during retirement. You have to be over 59 1/2, and you must have had the account for at least five years to get the benefit of tax-free withdrawals on earnings.

Still, in a pinch you can withdraw your Roth contributions without penalty or tax levy. You only tap your contributions. For example, let's say you put $3,000 into the Roth and suddenly you really need $1,000. You can take out the $1,000 and Uncle Sam won't tax you or penalize you. But if you withdraw any earnings, then a steep 10 percent fee and income tax hit apply.

A Roth has income restrictions. Single filers can qualify for the full contribution with a modified adjusted gross income of up to $105,000. You can make partial contributions up to an income of $120,000. For joint filers the comparable figures are up to $166,000 for a full contribution, with the amount phasing out at $176,000.

Stepping away from what you can't control and focusing on some of the things you can is taking advantage of the New Frugality to build a margin of safety. That's why the sustainability mantras that "less is more" and "enjoy the good things in life" will become as familiar as the slogans "Charge it" and "Do you take credit?"

Personal Finance

The margin-of-safety idea is most closely associated with Benjamin Graham, an investing legend. Graham was a pioneering investor, financial author, and teacher to generations of investors. His most famous student and acolyte is Warren Buffett, head of Berkshire Hathaway and best known as the Oracle of Omaha. Graham was born in London in 1894, and his family moved to the United States when he was young. The Grahams were poor, but he went to Columbia University, graduating in 1914. He ended up establishing an investment partnership, Graham-Newman, which racked up a stellar long-term record. He lectured at night at Columbia on finance and wrote several landmark investment books. "At a personal level, Graham was a caricature of the absent-minded professor, a devotee of the classics, a student of Latin and Greek, and a translator of Spanish poetry who could dress for work in mismatched shoes and who evidenced little interest in money," writes Roger Lowenstein, the finance author in a tribute essay to Benjamin Graham and David Dodd, co-authors of the investing bible *Security Analysis.* "It took Graham 20 years—which is to say, a complete cycle from the bull market of the Roaring Twenties through the dark, nearly ruinous days of the early 1930s—to refine his investment philosophy into a discipline that was as rigorous as the Euclidean theorems he had studied in college."

In *The Intelligent Investor*, his 1949 masterpiece, Graham memorably wrote, "In the old legend the wise men finally boiled down the history of mortal affairs into the single phrase, 'This too will pass.' Confronted with a like challenge to distill the secret of sound investment into three words, we venture the motto, MARGIN OF SAFETY." Graham always wanted to buy stocks for less than they were worth. He didn't want to pay too much for an investment, whether it was a bond, a stock, or a home. For instance, in 1973 the market value of the *Washington Post* was $80 million. Yet at the time Warren Buffett calculated that the assets—including the newspaper, *Newsweek* magazine, and a handful of television and radio stations—of the media company could be sold for at least $400 million. Buffett had a huge margin of safety even if his estimate was off. "You don't try and buy businesses worth $83 million for $80 million. You leave yourself an enormous margin," said Buffett in a 1984 talk. "When you build a bridge, you insist it can carry thirty thousand pounds, but you only drive ten-thousand-pound trucks across it. And that same principle works in investing."

With the benefit of hindsight, I came to appreciate the idea of a margin of safety after graduating from college. I went to sea, first getting my Coast Guard papers and later joining the Seafarers International Union. My first ship was a freighter that I caught in the summer of 1976 at the Brooklyn piers. My dad watched the ship get under way from his office at Waterman Steamship Corp. right across the river in Manhattan. But just as we steamed out of his vision, we hit another ship—a short voyage. I caught my next ship a few months later at Port Elizabeth, New Jersey. For the next seven months I worked on the SS *San Francisco*, shuttling between Europe and the Persian Gulf. Every morning I was awakened by

---

An Investment Risk Chart. My advice: Steer clear of high-risk assets

High risk: options, futures, collectibles

Medium risk: real estate, equity mutual funds, corporate bonds

Low risk: government bonds, bank savings accounts, CDs

a World War II veteran with the singsong phrase "Damn the submarine, we're the men of the merchant marine!"

The *San Francisco* was an old ship with a large crew in tight quarters. A tanker built for the U.S. Navy in 1941 (originally the *Chicopee*), it had ended up in the Pacific theater supplying fuel for the fleet in various operations, including Iwo Jima. The shipping company Sealand transformed it into a container ship two decades after the war, rechristening it the *San Francisco*. Container ships are massive cargo vessels that use special cranes to lift large steel, rectangular boxes off trucks and on board. The containers are delivered to another port, and the steel boxes are put on the backs of waiting trucks. The *San Francisco* still had its original giant boilers in the engine room where I worked. The crew quarters were from the same era. My job was engine-room wiper, the lowest rung among seamen working belowdecks. It's an accurate description, too, since I wiped up the engine room and cleaned the bathrooms. But I loved the job. It was an adventure.

I worked in the engine rooms of merchant ships on and off for four years, going through the Suez and Panama canals, steaming past the Rock of Gibraltar under a full moon at midnight, stopping in such ports as Athens, Dubai, Damman, Subic Bay, and Yokosuka. As a merchant seaman, you worked seven days a week with an eight-hour shift, plus four hours overtime Monday through Friday. The weekends were all overtime. The money in the late 1970s wasn't great, but there wasn't much to spend it on, either. Beer, cigarettes, and snacks from the ship's store, and more beer, more cigarettes, and more snacks when in port. Since time is money in the modern merchant marine, we never stayed long at any one dock, usually between twelve and forty-eight hours. I saved almost everything I earned at sea.

What money lessons did I learn in four years before the mast? First, never play poker with older seamen to pass the time drinking and talking night after night. It's an easy way to work every day for much of the year and walk down the gangway with empty pockets. (It is also a good idea to get along with a former marine "widow maker"— he took the point on foot patrol in Vietnam to disarm booby traps—and current motorcycle-gang member with a devil-worshipping girlfriend. But that's another story.) Second, I saw how planning and goals can pay off. A number of the seamen I met walked off the ships with little to show for it year after year. They spent what they earned onshore, then caught another ship to replenish their bank accounts. Yet on every voyage a handful had plans. They had done well with their money, buying a business for their spouse to run while they were at sea, investing the proceeds in homes to remodel with sweat equity between voyages, retiring to their home village in the Philippines or Yemen with a flush bank account, moving parents away from a crime-ridden Brooklyn neighborhood to safer streets. Somehow, some way, with work, with hustle, with a goal, some savings and a bet here and there, they believed tomorrow would be better than today.

Still, my main lesson was to appreciate the unknown when it comes to money or, perhaps more accurately, to embrace a margin of safety. After four years of working on and off ships, I took my savings and headed off to the London School of Economics to get a master's degree. I was flush. I made careful calculations that showed I had plenty of money to pay tuition, live well in London, and still have enough left over to pay for a job hunt back in the States.

I couldn't have been more wrong. Yes, the numbers worked for much of the year. But Jimmy Carter was president, America's inflation rate skyrocketed into double-digit territory, and the dollar kept reaching new lows against the British pound. The dramatic change in exchange rates eventually vaporized four years of labor and savings. Toward the end of my stay I was on a tight ramen-noodle diet. I returned to the States during a terrible recession nearly (but not quite) broke. Still, I'd do it again. After all, thanks to several years of working at sea and saving money, I got my degree, lived in London, and came home with no debt. It was worth it. But that cautionary experience informs the perspective of this book. My savings from my seafaring days were a margin of safety, but barely, it turned out to my chagrin.

Similarly, Angela's experience shows the importance of a cash cushion. I learned Angela's story when producer Lisa Blackstone interviewed

her for an episode of the public television show I hosted for several
years, *Right on the Money*. Angela was a freelance writer with a good career, reporting on health, fitness, and nutrition issues for women's magazines and writing books. In her early fifties around the time the dot-com
bubble burst, she owned her own home, had a retirement savings plan,
no debt (other than a mortgage), and excellent credit. "I'm not financially
sophisticated, but I think I have a lot of common sense," she said. "And to
me, finances seem simple in terms of not overextending yourself, not
overspending, keeping things within your limits, and bringing in more
than goes out."

She's right. Good thing, too, because that habit sheltered her from a
bad financial decision she had made several years earlier. Angela owned
a condo in Santa Monica, a town she loved. But she yearned for a home

---

Common pitfalls with managing money

Taking on credit card debt

Not saving

Waiting for tomorrow to save for retirement

Borrowing too much to buy a house, a car, a college
diploma

Avoiding taxes at all cost

Spending more than you earn

Going without a will

Not protecting your family with life insurance

Failing to shelter your earnings with disability insurance

Ignoring the cost of fees

and abruptly "made a well-meaning but ill-considered move." She sold her condo and bought a cabin in a ski resort outside Los Angeles. She says she had been seduced by the beauty of the countryside, the mountains, and the quiet. It wasn't long before she was bored and isolated. "I would sometimes go four or five days without speaking to anybody," she recalled. "There weren't a lot of cultural activities, and after three years I sold my house and moved back to the city."

Of course, Angela made a number of mistakes. She should have researched life in the mountains before selling her condo and rented a place in the countryside for an extended period to see if she really liked a rural existence. Nevertheless, she had left herself a considerable margin of safety, and when the move didn't work out, she could afford to reverse course.

Risk Matters

The word *risk* comes from the old Italian word, *risicare*, which means "to dare." "To dare reminds us that the essence of risk is about making decisions or choices with unknown outcomes," writes Peter Bernstein in *Against the Gods: The Remarkable Story of Risk.* "At its heart, risk management means considering the consequences of each choice we face."

Some of those choices will work out well. But some decisions will go bad. You'll make mistakes with your money. Everyone does. But you can prevent the consequences of choices that go wrong from being catastrophic by embracing a margin-of-safety perspective. Being conscious of the impact our financial choices—how we spend our money, earn our money, invest our money, and give it away—have on the environment and community will make the transition to the New Frugality lifestyle smoother.

CHAPTER 4

The New Frugality Rules

Straightforwardness and simplicity are in keeping with goodness.

—Seneca

THE SAVE-MORE-AND-BORROW-LESS MANTRA of the New Frugality signals a dramatic change from our past. We'll create a stronger balance sheet and a healthier lifestyle. The two overarching ideas, a margin of safety and sustainability, are critical. They feed off and support one another. Now it's time to lay out the key building blocks for getting your finances under control, to bring order out of the chaos. These are ideas I've settled on as vital after years of dealing with people's everyday money and value issues.

Keep It Simple

Simplicity is an underappreciated virtue with money. The risks and rewards of simple investments are easy to grasp and monitor. The expenses associated with such plain-vanilla offerings are low. It's easy to get into trouble buying investments and financial strategies we don't understand. Put it this way: Most complex financial products and cutting-edge money tactics manufactured by the financial-services industry have turned out to be bad for your financial health.

The same can't be said for the professionals. They have a hefty financial stake in selling complexity. Whether it's with an insurance policy loaded up with all kinds of bells and whistles, an investment strategy that only a tenured mathematician can grasp, or a clever estate plan that dazzles the legal fraternity, the pros are pocketing lush profits selling supposed sophistication. Certainly, high fees reduce returns. That's the case with many retirement savings plans. Take this example from the Congressional Research Service. It looked at U.S. stock and bond market returns over an eighty-year period, from 1926 through 2005. Based on that market history, a couple earning the median income and contributing 6 percent of family earnings each year for thirty years into a 401(k) account invested two-thirds in stocks and one-third in bonds could expect to accumulate $356,434 (in inflation-adjusted dollars). That figure also assumes that the 401(k) expenses are equal to 0.4 percent of plan assets. But if the annual expenses were equal to 2 percent of plan assets, the couple would face retirement with only $263,663, or 26 percent less.

I've always liked the way Warren Buffett illustrates the fee-complexity dynamic. He created the "Gotrocks" family. The Gotrocks owned all of Corporate America, worth about $700 billion. They spent some on pleasure, but mostly they allowed their investments to appreciate. But a few "fast-talking Helpers" convinced each family member to let them manage the money—for a price—with the promise of doing better than their relatives. Who could resist? Problem is, no one did well. Another set of Helpers came in, money managers. The pie kept getting smaller. Financial planners and institutional consultants were hired to pick the money managers. So it went as "Wall Street's Pied Pipers of Performance" kept charging more and doing worse, all in the futile pursuit of achieving above-average performance. "Call this promise the adult version of Lake Wobegon," says Buffett.

Another reason for keeping it simple is how busy we all are today. We don't have the time to become a financial specialist, and most of us don't want to spend hours managing our money. We work hard for our money. Employers demand a lot of effort on our part. We not only work, we raise families, spend time with friends, and volunteer in the community. Our expectations of ourselves have gone up, too. We try to eat a healthy diet, get regular exercise, and keep up with the latest technologies. "We now believe that many things are necessary for our physical, mental, and emotional well-being," says Joel Mokyr, an economic historian at Northwestern University. Adds Ronald C. Jepperson, sociologist at Tulsa University, "The definition of a full life has become extremely full."

Simplicity also means knowing yourself. An approach to money that does wonders for a colleague or neighbor may not be suited to your temperament or circumstances. For instance, in the nineties I tried and failed at maintaining a budget on various software programs. I learned that it was much easier for me to keep track of household money with a pen, a notebook, and a calculator. That is, until the latest generation of online budget programs came out. I find them comfortable to use. Similarly, most advisers will recommend including a healthy dose of equities in a long-term retirement savings portfolio. That advice owes a big debt to research by the Nobel laureate Paul Samuelson. Yet in an interview I had with him he emphasized whether you included equities in a portfolio depended on your attitude toward stock market risk. "For my late mother, her level of risk tolerance called for a very small equity share," he said.

One of my favorite stories's for illustrating the importance of knowing yourself involves J. P. Morgan, the great nineteenth-century financier. The tale goes that a man was in a panic after putting all his money into the stock market. He wanted to be rich, but if the stock market crashed, he was financially ruined. He couldn't sleep. One day, seeing the imposing figure of Morgan on a street, he summoned up his courage, and asked, "Mr. Morgan, I've invested all my money in the stock market and I can't sleep. I'm a wreck. What should I do?"

Morgan replied, "Sell down to the sleeping point."

What is your sleeping point?

You want to control your money. You don't want your money to control you. Stick to what is simple. You'll be better off financially and you'll have more time for the important things in life.

Pay Yourself First

This is another way of saying, save. There's no getting around it. Saving means making trade-offs. Mick Jagger was right when he sang, "You Can't Always Get What You Want."

Whenever you make a decision to do something—such as save—you foreclose other options. Economists call the value of the goods and services you sacrificed in making a choice an "opportunity cost." It's a measure (albeit an imprecise one) of what we have given up. It helps us better understand the return we expect from our choices. For instance, the late Robert Eisner, an economist at Northwestern University, somewhat tongue in cheek illustrated opportunity cost this way. The cost of buying and reading his book—*The Misunderstood Economy*—was not only the dollars spent on it, but also the value of the time spent reading it and the alternative use of that time. In other words, his book should only be read if you believe your return, both in enlightenment and enjoyment, exceeds its opportunity cost, that is, money spent on the book and the time required to read it.

The concept of opportunity cost—the principle that you have to make choices in using your time and resources—is important when thinking about paying yourself first. For instance, a retirement savings plan at work or that you set up on your own is a great way to save. Your money grows sheltered from taxes until you withdraw it in old age. The savings will make a huge difference in your standard of living years from now. Still, many people find it tough to participate. Yet not saving in a retirement plan is a huge mistake. Even if money is tight you should put in just a few dollars out of every paycheck. You can always increase the contributions later on if your pay or circumstances improve.

But what you can't get back is time, and it is by taking advantage of time that even small contributions grow into large sums. For instance, suppose you open up an Individual Retirement Account (IRA) at age twenty. You put $1,000 a year into an IRA until age thirty. You then stop. You only contributed to the IRA for ten years. When you retire at age sixty-five you'll have $168,514 in the account, assuming you earned 7 percent on your money. Now, let's say you didn't start investing in an IRA until you were thirty, but this time you put $1,000 a year into the account until age sixty-five. You faithfully invest for thirty-five years. However, your nest egg is worth only $147,913, or $20,601 less, assuming a 7 percent rate of return.

You can play with the numbers and the assumptions, but the message remains the same: The earlier you start saving the better the odds of making good money over the years. It's why you want to just say no to debt and focus on building up your savings.

Savings suggestions from "Bud"

In 1956, Henry K. "Bud" Hebeler left Boston with a graduate degree in engineering from MIT for a job at Boeing in Seattle. Some three decades after he made that trip in a Volkswagen Beetle, he retired as president of the company's giant aerospace unit. It wasn't long before Hebeler started a new career dispensing conservative financial advice on his Web site, analyzenow.com. You're not going to agree with all of these suggestions, but it will get you thinking.

- Decide how much you should be saving as the first step. (Web sites can help with this.)

- Establish a lower family budget that satisfies your savings goal and stay within it.

- Arrange for automatic savings deposits from your paychecks.

- Sell things you don't really need on the Net or elsewhere.

- Downsize your home or rent. Renting provides mobility to get jobs elsewhere in the country.

- Move in with relatives or friends.

- Grow your own vegetables.

- Buy items with cash, not with loans.

- Rule out cars, cell phones, or iPods for children—or even for yourselves.

- Make do with old computers, and software. Use no downloads requiring payments.

- Try to get lower-cost TV, Internet, and telephone services.

- Turn down the thermostat and wear sweaters.

- Consider refinancing your mortgage if interest rates are now significantly lower.

- Older people may not need life insurance or long-term-care insurance.

The trade-off to save more is worth it. You can come up with different scenarios, but here's an illustration I like from economist Robert Frank of Cornell. He compared the total consumption of a big saver versus a big spender over a lifetime. From age twenty-one to retirement at age sixty-six, the saver and the spender each make $50,000 a year with no pay increases. (Examples like this are often unrealistic to draw out the point.) The high spender starting at age twenty-one spends all his money every year. He makes a $9,000 credit card purchase at age twenty-one and pays 20 percent on it, or $1,800 a year. He pays off the credit card debt at retirement. Savings are zero, too. In sharp contrast, the saver puts 20 percent of total income—including the 5 percent earned on money—into savings. The savings account balance at retirement is $564,811. The saver has less money to spend compared to the spender from ages twenty-one to forty. But from age forty to sixty-six she has more than her annual income of $50,000 a year to spend, peaking at well over $60,000 at age sixty-six.

You should pay yourself first into two broad categories. The first group of savings is in taxable accounts, such as savings accounts, certificates of deposit, and mutual funds. This is your emergency savings, your opportunity fund, and long-term savings that can be cashed in at some point without incurring a financial penalty. I would "automate" this savings by arranging to have money regularly withdrawn from your checking account. The second category of savings is to take advantage of tax-sheltered retirement plans, such as a 401(k) and IRA.

How much should you save? There are no hard-and-fast rules. The standard rule of thumb was to salt away some 10 percent to 15 percent of income. In recent years that figure has been upped to 15 percent to 20 percent, largely reflecting greater income insecurity and rising health care costs. However, what's really important is to get started. Putting any percent of your gross income into savings will do at first. The notion that saving more means penury is wrong with time—and by time I don't mean extremely old age. You'll still be young enough to enjoy it.

Invest in Yourself

I want to expand the definition of savings beyond Treasury bills and equity mutual funds. Our most important investment is in our education and career, skills and knowledge—what economists call human capital. The returns on human capital include your income from your job and Social Security (which is based on your earnings history). It includes the skills you need to advance in your career, or to embark on a new venture. "A raw human being has about as much economic value as an uncultivated piece of land in the wilderness," writes Fischer Black, the late financial genius. "Through his own efforts and through the efforts of others, a person takes on education, socialization, and experience that increase his economic value just as surely as roads, sewers, utilities, and buildings increase the value of a piece of land."

For most of us, the bulk of our wealth comes from our job. Economists estimate that the lifetime rate of return on a four-year college education is between 10 percent and 15 percent annually. It's not just college. Training, specific-industry seminars, and other lifelong learning programs pay off. It is worth it to develop networks, too. The more connections you've developed over the years the more you'll get paid and the greater your opportunities, according to research by Nobel laureate Kenneth Arrow and Federal Reserve economist Ron Borzekowski.

What's more, we're living longer, healthier lives. A seismic shift in the economy and workplace is making it easier for an aging population to work. An information- and services-dominated economy will ease the transition to more years of employment. Simply put, toiling away on a computer in medical diagnostics or government bureaucracy is far less demanding than manning an auto assembly line or mining for gold. Investing in knowledge is critical for managing career shifts throughout life, well into the golden years. "I think we are going to see much more emphasis put on preparing for second careers, for example, and part-time employment in one's older years, more flexible patterns of employment over one's lifetime," says Zvi Bodie, finance professor at Boston University.

Worry About the Downside

One of the most powerful ways to protect your finances from catastrophe is to diversify. The basic idea is simple. As Miguel de Cervantes put it in *Don Quixote* some four hundred years ago, "It is the part of a wise man to keep himself today for tomorrow, and not venture all his eggs in one basket." Shakespeare illustrated the concept of diversification around the same time in *The Merchant of Venice*, when Antonio told his friends he wasn't spending sleepless nights worrying over his commodity investment:

> *Believe me, no. I thank my fortune for it,*
> *My ventures are not in one bottom trusted,*
> *Nor to one place; nor is my whole estate*
> *Upon the fortune of this present year.*
> *Therefore my merchandise makes me not sad.*

An axiom of modern finance is that the only way to create the opportunity to earn a higher return is to take greater risks—and vice versa. The trick is to mix and match the major financial-market assets to create a well-diversified portfolio. When some assets, such as a home and stocks, zig, other assets, such as bonds and money market funds, might zag. The

Common investing mistakes

Lack of a financial plan or investment strategy

Failure to diversify

Following the crowd

Acting on tips or market-timing advice

Not paying attention to cost

Short-term thinking

Chasing returns while ignoring risk

Selecting investments without taking into account your time horizon

Failure to admit mistakes

concept of diversification goes further. It is a way to limit the risk of getting fleeced by a Bernie Madoff, the convicted crook who masterminded the largest Ponzi scheme in history. Some of his victims lost everything. Among them was Elie Wiesel, the Holocaust survivor and Nobel Peace Prize recipient. Not only was his charitable foundation wiped out by Madoff, but so was his personal wealth. "All of a sudden, everything we have done in forty years—literally, my books, my lectures, my university salary, everything—was gone," Wiesel said at the time.

To be sure, diversification doesn't offer investors much protection during extraordinary financial crisis, such as during the recessions of 2007–09 and 1973–74. The financial carnage is widespread. This is where another related technique for managing risk comes into play. It's called "hedging." With a hedge you give up some potential for growth in your portfolio in return for maintaining a minimum level of wealth. A classic hedging investment is U.S. Treasuries, including short-term Treasury bills and Treasury Inflation Protected Securities or TIPS. For example, Professor Bodie is a leading proponent of ensuring a minimum standard of living in old age by investing the bulk of retirement savings in TIPS. Another example of a hedge is putting money into a bank savings account or certificate of deposit insured by the Federal Deposit Insurance Corporation or FDIC. So long as you are under the insurance limits, your money is safe even if the bank fails. Indeed, no one with an FDIC-insured account has lost a penny from a bank failure since the government's insurance fund was created in 1933.

In a famous essay, "The Hedgehog and the Fox," British philosopher Sir Isaiah Berlin examines this sentence by the Greek poet Archilochus: "The fox knows many things, but the hedgehog one big thing." Berlin believes that sentence captures a great intellectual divide. "For there exists a great chasm between those, on the one side, who relate everything to a single central vision, one system less or more coherent or articulate . . . And, on the other side, those who pursue many ends often unrelated and even contradictory, connected, if at all, only in some de facto way . . . The first kind of intellectual and artistic personality belongs to the hedgehogs, the second to the foxes."

Investing tends to attract hedgehogs. But hedgehogs beware. Remember when high-tech stocks were a surefire investment in the 1990s? How about real estate in the 2000s? Investing is an activity for philosophical relativists. And that means diversification pays.

Borrow Rarely and Wisely

Debt is potentially dangerous. For far too many young people personal finance has meant getting out of debt, from credit cards to student loans. Middle-aged workers are burdened by their mortgages and home-equity loans. And more seniors than ever are carrying steep debt burdens into their retirement years.

It would be easy to say, don't borrow. I'd like to write that. But that's the wrong lesson to take from the recent debacle. Instead, the message is if you do have to borrow be "conservative and wise."

My strong belief is that we should only take on debts that add to our economic choices and quality of life. For instance, most of us can't afford to buy a home and earn a college degree without taking on debt. Both of these investments offer a return over time. Still, you should weigh the risks and be conservative with your borrowing. For instance, I wouldn't purchase a home unless you can put 20 percent down and qualify for a plain-vanilla low-cost mortgage. Similarly, a college loan can be a wonderful investment over a lifetime. But you don't want to fall into a stressful situation where it's tough to pay back the loan. A traditional benchmark is that no more than 8 percent of a college graduate's income should go toward paying off student loans.

No matter how tempting, and the lure is strong, credit cards shouldn't be used to spend more than you make. The bill should be paid off monthly. It's not just credit cards. Your home is not an ATM. You want to take a vacation you can afford, not a trip you can't pay for without taking out a home-equity loan. A six-year auto loan may offer low monthly payments but the total cost of the bill is too steep. Buy a cheaper car.

The goal is to be debt free over time, and the younger you can be without debt the better. Paying off debt is as important as setting aside savings. Both actions are good habits that provide a strong margin of safety. However, it's especially important to be debt free when entering your retirement years. There is no reason to have to deal with the pressure of mortgage payments at that stage in life.

Give Back

You can't control the business cycle, the ups and downs of the economy. You can't predict the timing of the next bear or bull market. You can take thoughtful steps to shore up your community. You can control your giving, your volunteering and service to others. Giving back is a core part of any long-term financial plan, much like investing for retirement or saving for your children's college education. It sustains the community and it lets us know that we aren't alone. "Money is to be spent or given away," says Ross Levin, a certified financial planner and president of Accredited Investors Inc. in Edina, Minnesota. "Planned, systemic giving to charity helps dislodge the hold that money may have over you. Sharing your experiences and hopes can have a huge impact on those around you. You get to choose to make a difference."

Caring and giving is the essence of sustainability.

Think Big

You don't want get lost in the minutiae of personal finance. It's important to figure out how to divide your 401(k) money into equities and bonds or if it makes sense for you to leave your brick-and-mortar bank for an online competitor. Still, it pays to step back every once in a while and ask yourself the big questions, such as, where do I want to be a year, five years, ten years from now? Is this the right career for me or is it time to explore another path? What about that dream I've always had in the back of my mind? Should I let it go, or go for it? As Woody Allen wisely remarked, "Life isn't a dress rehearsal—it's reality."

In other words you need a plan. Your goals and desires will change over time. Yet even a loose plan helps keep you focused. Talk about your ideas with friends and family. A margin of financial safety lets you experiment, try different things, and get back on track after a setback. And don't forget to take your dreams seriously. Sometimes it takes a while to get there.

Just ask the hot-dog man. I met him at a square in downtown Boulder, Colorado. A somewhat rakish, charismatic white-haired man was selling hot dogs behind his cart, yelling out in a loud cadence, "Hot dog, hot dog, hot dog, Pepsi, Pepsi, chips, chips." He did a great business and clearly enjoyed himself. He was born and raised in Chicago, about a mile walk from Wrigley Field. His folks would let him go to day games by himself

Your net worth. Do you know it? I'll bet most of you don't. Go ahead, hazard a guess. Jot it down. You can see how you did later on after you've figured out the actual number. I get lost a lot driving around town. I always think I know where I am going, and I often don't have a clue. It's time to get out the map. Your net worth is the financial equivalent of that map.

In theory, the net worth equation is simple. You add up the value of your home, your retirement savings plans, your savings accounts, and any asset that could be sold and turned into cash. You then tally up everything you owe, from your mortgage to your car loan to the balance you carry on a credit card. Your net worth is your assets minus those liabilities.

Of course, the basic idea may be simple, but it takes a lot of time and effort to gather all the information. Your record keeping might be a bit haphazard. The good news is that there are plenty of worksheets in the library or bookstore to help guide you. Even better are the online resources—sites like Mint.com and networthiq.com—that are increasingly easy to use and update.

The net worth calculation gives you a good idea of how you're doing overall. If you have more assets than liabilities you have what's called a positive net worth. Congratulations. It signals a healthy household balance sheet. Better yet, it could mean that you have the means to take sensible risks. You have a negative net worth if the total amount you owe is more than you own. One advantage of figuring out your net worth is that it forces you not to ignore the bad stuff.

Take this scenario: You have a healthy investment portfolio and a good credit score. But you've taken out a second mortgage, carry a hefty balance on your credit cards, and have some private student loans. Your net worth is likely negative. That's a good indication you're vulnerable to a setback—like a job loss or a medical illness.

A few years ago many people didn't worry about their net worth. Their stock portfolio was up. Their home had appreciated. You could afford to borrow lots of money, right? Wrong. The unhappy history of recent events proves it's vital to have an accurate gauge of your overall financial health.

There's nothing magical about the net worth number. No one calculation is the "best." The reason I like net worth is that gathering the data and knowing your net worth forces you to grapple with all aspects of your financial life. It's a critical database or foundation for sensible financial planning.

from the time he was eight. He recalled two old hot-dog sellers, one on the corner of Addison and Sheffield and the other on the corner of Waveland Avenue and Clark Street. These are the corners that are alongside Wrigley Field. "These guys were old Armenian guys, which is my national heritage," he said. "They were friends of my grandfather, and they had the two hot-dog stands. And I'd go there and I'd get hot dogs all the time. I'd look at them, put that lower lip out. And they'd say, 'You want a hot dog?' I'd say, 'Yeah.' And they'd give me a hog dog. I'd run like hell to the other side. I'd do that three, four, five times a game. And I always, always wanted to have a hot-dog stand. My mother used to say when other kids wanted to be firemen or cowboys or policemen or whatever, I wanted to have a hot-dog stand."

Well, he worked for Anheuser-Busch for some four decades, owning a piece of a beer distributorship. He loved his job and supported his family. At age fifty-seven, he retired from the beer business. But he remembered the dream of owning a hot-dog stand. He took some savings, bought a stand, and opened for business. He was obviously successful in his new career, with a long line of customers. But he took a moment to reflect. "Everybody always has a hot-dog stand in the back of their mind, whether it's painting mailboxes or découpage, whatever. Everybody has that. Enjoy yourself going through the process of thinking about how you would set that up. Because that's half the fun. You always want to follow your heart, if you will. But sometimes it's difficult. And you have to face reality sometimes."

He loves what he does. What is *your* hot-dog stand?

There you have it, the main ideas behind my approach to personal finance. The overarching New Frugality concepts are the interplay between creating a margin of financial safety and living a life that is mindful of sustainability values. The practical insights that support this approach are: Keep it simple; pay yourself first; invest in yourself; worry about the downside; borrow rarely and wisely; give back; and think big. These concepts reflect some three decades of experience covering personal finance and economics. I also learned them the hard way, from carrying a large credit card debt burden to forgetting to focus on the hot-dog stand.

CHAPTER 5

Make Frugality a Habit

The noblest question in the world is, What good may I do in it?

—Benjamin Franklin

"DON'T SPEND MORE THAN YOU EARN" is an insight from the ages. The thirteenth-century architect, mathematician, artist and Renaissance intellectual Leon Battista Alberti cautioned, "Your expenditure should never exceed your income."

The nineteenth-century novelist Charles Dickens memorably captured the same sentiment in *David Copperfield*. The kindly but debt-ridden Mr. Wilkins Micawber advised a young David Copperfield, "Annual income twenty pounds, annual expenditure nineteen six, result happiness. Annual income twenty pounds, annual expenditure twenty pounds ought and six, result misery."

Sadly, Dickens knew what he was writing about since his father had been sent to the debtors' prison. So, let's delve into the basics of building a solid financial foundation for your household. The focus of this chapter will be on finding the money that can be used to pay off debts and build savings. I'll also extend the concept of financial security to include insurance and wills.

Compound Interest

The money you set aside grows over time. It builds on a simple, but powerful dynamic, what Albert Einstein is said to have called the "most powerful force in the universe": compound interest.

Here's the basic idea. Let's say you deposit $1,000 in a bank and you earn 3 percent interest. At the end of the year, you have $1,030. You earn 3 percent the following year, but now it's off $1,030. You end up with $1,061. By year three, the figure grows to $1,093. And so on.

Here's my favorite example for illustrating the power of compound interest. In a 1930 essay, the economist John Maynard Keynes wrote that the value of Great Britain's foreign investments was about £4 billion. He traced the beginnings of that money to the treasure Sir Francis Drake stole from Spain in 1580. Drake's plunder was enough to let Queen Elizabeth pay off England's foreign debt, balance the budget, and invest £40,000 in the Levant Company (with profits invested in the East India Company). "Now it happens that £40,000 accumulating at $3^1/4$ per cent compound interest approximately corresponds to the actual volume of England's foreign investments at various dates, and would actually amount today to the total of £4,000,000,000 which I have already quoted as being what our foreign investments now are," he writes. "Thus, every £1 which Drake brought home in 1580 has now become £100,000. Such is the power of compound interest!"

Compound interest is how the financial turtle can beat the money hare. Even small sums of money add up. Compound interest is why creating a margin of safety is easier than it may appear.

Automate Your Savings

The simplest, most effective way to pay yourself first and tap into the power of compound interest is to "automate" savings. Anyone participating in an employer-sponsored retirement savings plan, such as a 401(k), 403(b), or 457 has the money automatically taken out of every paycheck.

You can do the same thing with your checking account, even if it's $10, $25, $50, or $100 every month. The money you automatically put into savings won't look like much at first, but it will grow over time.

It's intriguing to note that William Whyte in his piece on budgetism in the 1950s surmised that the same installment-debt dynamic could work to build savings. "So far budgetism, has operated largely to put

Thanks to compound interest, a twenty-four-year-old who saves even small amounts of money will see a nice gain over time. The higher the interest rate, the better the return, too.

$2 PER DAY...OR $730 A YEAR COMPOUNDING MONTHLY PAYMENT OF $61 AT 2% WILL BE WORTH	$5 PER DAY...OR $1825 A YEAR COMPOUNDING MONTHLY PAYMENT OF $152 AT 2% WILL BE WORTH
$8,100 in 10 years	$20,200 in 10 years
$18,000 in 20 years	$44,900 in 20 years
$30,100 in 30 years	$75,100 in 30 years
AT 4% WILL BE WORTH	**AT 4% WILL BE WORTH**
$9,000 in 10 years	$22,500 in 10 years
$22,400 in 20 years	$55,900 in 20 years
$42,400 in 30 years	$105,800 in 30 years
AT 6% WILL BE WORTH	**AT 6% WILL BE WORTH**
$10,000 in 10 years	$25,000 in 10 years
$28,300 in 20 years	$70,600 in 20 years
$61,600 in 30 years	$153,500 in 30 years

more people in debt, but there is nothing inherent in the process that requires it to do that," he writes. "Budgetism, essentially, is a person's desire to regularize his income by having it removed from his own control and disciplined by external forces. But could not this urge be applied to savings, too?" Yes, it can, and it should be in all your savings, from an emergency fund to a retirement savings plan.

This is all very good, but where will the money come from? It's time to focus on frugality: making changes in your spending habits that are sustainable and green so that you have discretionary income to save.

Where's the Money?

Did you ever read the popular children's book series *Where's Waldo?* You look at complicated, colorful cartoons and try to find Waldo. It's a bit like that with developing habits of frugality. You look around, try things out, and see what works. You're not alone, either. Lots of people in your neighborhood, in your community, and in online social networks are sharing ideas and passing on their experiences with frugality and sustainability. Tap into those conversations.

What are some tricks of the frugality trade? Many of the techniques are time-honored, updated for the Internet age. Clip coupons. Watch for sales. Trim cable, cell-phone, and Internet costs. Don't pay ATM fees. Find no-fee checking and savings accounts. In the winter, turn down the thermostat, and in the summer, use ceiling fans instead of air-conditioning. Feed your family home-cooked meals and take the leftovers for your lunch at work. Reduce. Reuse. Recycle.

Visit thrift stores and consignment shops instead of the Gap and Target. All of us—most of us—have stuff we've bought and no longer need, or things that we never needed. Much of the stuff is in good shape. You can sell it. You can give it away to charity. Or you can tap into one of the free recycling communities that are springing up all over the country. You can easily find and join a recycling network online. One of the better known is Freecycle, and communities like it are growing fast. These sites

The Internet is a great resource for frugality ideas. Of course, blogs come and go, as do Web sites. Here are some Internet resources I've enjoyed exploring and using to learn about eco-friendly frugality. I've picked a range of sites; some blogs focus primarily on one person's views, while others gather information from a variety of sources.

frugalliving.about.com

frugalvillage.net

sustainablog.org

worldchanging.org

simple-green-frugal.blogspot.com

1greengeneration.elementsintime.com

greendaily.com

inhabitat.com

green.yahoo.com

greenerpenny.com

freecycle.org

treehugger.com

greenmoneyjournal.com

slowfoodusa.org

let people post items they don't want and look for stuff that they do. These free recycling communities have individual rules, but among the items that work well for giving away are furniture, especially children's furniture, mobile homes, lawn equipment, toys, and clothing.

Many of these money-saving strategies are embraced during a recession or when our household income drops sharply from a job loss. We all cut back on spending during lean times. The idea is to maintain frugal habits all the time, good times and bad.

One way to do that is to experiment and learn what fits with your lifestyle. For instance, I became intrigued by the cost trade-off between a clothesline and a dryer. I grew up with a clothesline; my mom never used a dryer. But I did. Here's how I did the calculation: I could buy a new retractable clothesline on the Internet for about $10. The price of running a dryer load is about 34 cents. (That figure will vary depending on where you live, energy prices, and the kind of dryer you own.) Anyway, I do a load of wash once a week. It would take me almost thirty weeks to equal the cost of the clothesline. It's all savings after that. Small sums add up over time, right?

For some people, using a clothesline is a smart, frugal move. I tried it, but it wasn't really practical for me in my two-bedroom apartment. It made the apartment feel small and crowded, and using some racks had the same effect. The experiment is over, and I'm back to bundling up my laundry and walking over to the nearby Laundromat. It's a nice neighborhood meeting place. Other frugal and green habits are easier for me to adopt. I love bookstores. My bookshelves are full with Scandinavian mysteries, economic history, social commentary, and the like. These days my friends and I are sharing books. For me, it's both frugal and fun. As much as I miss having a copy of every book I read on my shelf, I love the conversations I have with friends about the books we've swapped. Of course, these are very small steps. I'll get into some bigger money-saving and green strategies later on. Still, I'm convinced that little experiments and small shifts in behavior end up having a noticeable impact on our ecological footprint and our savings accounts.

Planning Is Crucial

It's easier to be frugal with research and forethought. We all end up spending more when we're rushed, make travel plans at the last minute, or even go to the grocery store in a hurry. Planning is a constant theme in the frugality literature. Here's a small but telling example. I've known Karen and Orton Tofte for more than three decades, and for the past several years we've met every Saturday for coffee. They're incredibly generous. They had nothing when they were newlyweds living on Minnesota's North Shore, far up Lake Superior. Karen used to make clothes for their two young daughters out of Orton's old, frayed sweaters, and she even cut up her wedding dress to make homespun clothing. Among the many good money habits they developed—and maintained—from those years are three easy ones to copy: They take out a certain amount of cash each week for spending; they come up with menus for the week; and they cook enough to have leftovers for lunch the next day—and no more. Again, with planning it's easy to put aside a few dollars here and a few dollars there. Eventually you have savings where before you had an empty bank account.

The combination of frugality, sustainability, planning, and thoughtfully developing the money-saving habits that reflect your values will prevent the "don't spend more than you earn" perspective from turning into cheapness. There is nothing attractive about being cheap. It's why many of the thrift ideas shrilly pushed during economic downturns are quickly abandoned as the economy improves. Frugality isn't about extreme denial and shrunken ambitions. For instance, Amy Dacyczyn became the guru of thrift during the recession of the early 1990s. She was famous for the *Tightwad Gazette*, her monthly newsletter "Promoting Thrift as a Viable Alternative Lifestyle."

Sounds good, right? Her newsletter spawned a cult following. But here is how she described herself in the inaugural 1990 issue of the *Gazette*:

"I am a compulsive tightwad. People who know me believe that I worry too much about money, that I don't spend enough on myself, and that I don't know how to have any fun. Even Depression-era relatives think that I am too thrifty. One Christmas an aunt gave me two boxes of aluminum foil after learning that I reused the stuff. (I made one box last for two years.) And when I was first labeled 'The Frugal Zealot' even I had to smile . . . I became a reuser first of aluminum foil, then of Ziploc bags, and now, I publicly confess, I have become a reuser of vacuum cleaner bags. (No Christmas presents please.)"

We shouldn't scoff too quickly: Dacyczyn did raise six children, buy a large house, and save a sizable nest egg on her husband's modest salary. But you can accomplish similar goals without going to such extremes. Being frugal doesn't mean reusing your vacuum bags, I promise. Still, Dacyczyn was onto something: You can tell from her writing she made cheapness into a game. In the same way, we can learn to enjoy the skills and satisfaction of frugal living. This time, frugal habits will stick with us.

Downsize

Sometimes you need to make a bigger break in your spending pattern to boost savings or pay down debt. The answer: downsize.

It works. I was living in a comfortable two-bedroom apartment, but it was too expensive. I had finally adopted many of the frugal habits I've discussed, although it took me a while to get there. I don't know about you, but it always takes longer to bring about changes than I imagine or hope. What works for me is to take small steps and build on those rather than moving too quickly. Anyway, I realized that I needed to take stronger action to save more. I moved to a smaller two-bedroom apartment where the rent was nearly half my previous monthly carry. My finances improved even more because my monthly energy costs were dramatically less.

The same dynamic holds for homeowners. Yes, the housing market is a mess. But Anne in Olivebridge, New York, was thinking ahead. "I'm 50 yrs old and have been thinking about downsizing and relocating for a few years now. I am self-employed and can take my work with me, so my income is not tied to a particular location," she e-mailed. "My plan is to sell my current home, of which I own about 70%, and take that cash to buy a different house that would better suit my needs as I age, etc." I didn't think what she was contemplating was a "foolish endeavor" at all. Small homes are financially smart. Large homes cost significantly more to maintain. Property taxes are higher. The savings from running a small home compound over time. Plus, as we age, most of us are less inclined or able to do maintenance. Smaller yards and single-story homes become much more attractive, as do condominiums and townhomes where maintenance is contracted out.

When it comes to housing, going green is no longer reserved for the income elite. The surge in demand for energy-efficient and ecologically friendly homes is up, despite all the turmoil in the housing market in recent years. In a classic case from economics 101, increased demand has induced bigger supply. The larger market is driving down prices on green construction materials and design. The government has passed a variety of tax incentives to encourage more green home investment. Green walls, ceilings, and windows are designed for better energy efficiency. Green homes also consume less water than conventional homes, mostly by installing water-efficient appliances, and storing rainwater for irrigation. "We have passed the tipping point for builders going green," Harvey M. Bernstein, vice president at McGraw-Hill Construction, said at an industry conference. Added Ray Tonjes, chair of the Green Building Subcommittee for the National Association of Home Builders, at the same conference, "It's official. Green has gone mainstream."

Transportation

When it comes to transportation in the United States, we're mostly talking cars in most parts of the country. Where possible, it's frugal to use public transportation, bike, and walk. Scooters and small-bore motorcycles are increasingly popular. More people are giving up their car these days, too. Bravo. That isn't practical for many people, at least not yet. There are still car savings to be had. Hybrid cars, electric cars, and highly fuel-efficient vehicles are doing well with consumers. It's good for the wallet. The appeal of these kinds of cars will only grow, especially as the spread of strong economic growth into the world's major emerging markets will continue to put upward pressure on the price of oil and gas. But are hybrids and alternative-energy cars really green? After all, cars and the sprawling infrastructure of roads that support them are a major impediment toward reducing our carbon footprint. It's an important point to keep in mind, but I still think the embrace of fuel-thrifty cars is part of a broader wave of ecological consciousness and sustainable actions. The greening of America is happening on a very personal and financial level. It builds on itself, gathering momentum from steps taken at home, on the road, at work, and in our spending and investing choices. The shift in car buying habits from gas-guzzlers to fuel-sippers is a critical part of that overall process.

Full disclosure: I don't really understand the workings of cars. You turn the ignition, put the car in gear, push down on the peddle, and drive off. That's about as far as my knowledge goes. To my sons' disgust, I own a car with a stick shift because it was cheaper. My car is also fuel efficient (they like that).

A car is expensive. It isn't just the price of gasoline. The cost of ownership includes auto insurance, depreciation, and maintenance and repairs. If you borrowed to buy the car, add the cost of the loan or lease. During the Great Recession many people decided to keep driving their current car rather than buy a new one. It's a smart move that saves money. The time to get rid of the car is when the cost of repairs starts rising sharply.

Downsizing is a savvy move when it comes to cars. Fuel economy pays. It reduces your carbon footprint. And the less you end up going to the gas station, the less money drains out of your pocket.

If you can, it's always cheapest to buy a car with cash. If you can't afford an all-cash purchase, borrow as little as possible for a short period of time. I'd steer clear of any loan longer than three years. What about the question of new versus used? A new car is much more expensive than used. Yet with a new car and comprehensive warranty you should get at

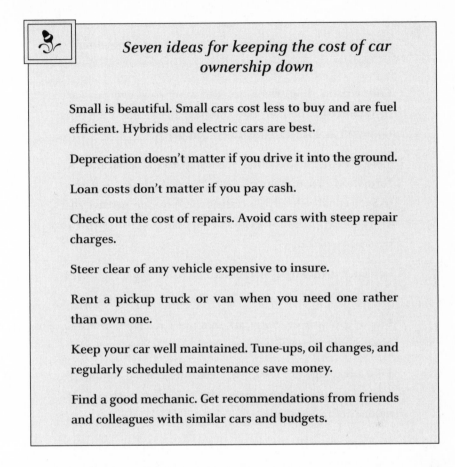

Seven ideas for keeping the cost of car ownership down

Small is beautiful. Small cars cost less to buy and are fuel efficient. Hybrids and electric cars are best.

Depreciation doesn't matter if you drive it into the ground.

Loan costs don't matter if you pay cash.

Check out the cost of repairs. Avoid cars with steep repair charges.

Steer clear of any vehicle expensive to insure.

Rent a pickup truck or van when you need one rather than own one.

Keep your car well maintained. Tune-ups, oil changes, and regularly scheduled maintenance save money.

Find a good mechanic. Get recommendations from friends and colleagues with similar cars and budgets.

least three trouble-free years of driving. For many people, that is enough of a reason to buy new. Another advantage of a new car is that it allows you to take advantage of the most fuel-efficient options on the road. For others, the cost savings from buying used are simply too great to pass up. I've sort of evaded the issue by buying new and driving the car into the ground.

If you do decide to buy a used car, the good news is that it's a much improved market. It wasn't all that long ago that the terms "lemon" and "unscrupulous" were synonymous with "used car" and "used car dealer." Author Roald Dahl in the children's book *Matilda* had the girl's miserable father

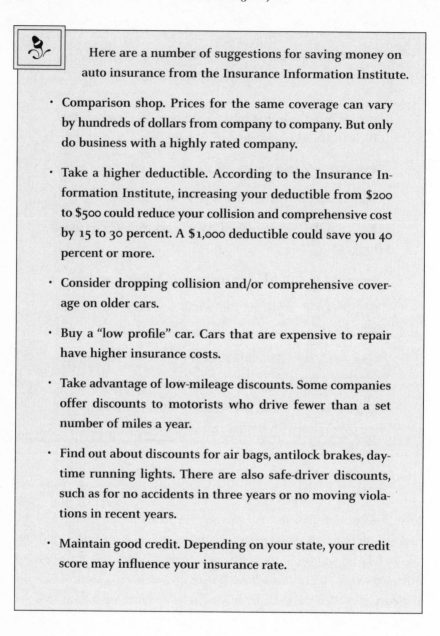

Here are a number of suggestions for saving money on auto insurance from the Insurance Information Institute.

- Comparison shop. Prices for the same coverage can vary by hundreds of dollars from company to company. But only do business with a highly rated company.

- Take a higher deductible. According to the Insurance Information Institute, increasing your deductible from $200 to $500 could reduce your collision and comprehensive cost by 15 to 30 percent. A $1,000 deductible could save you 40 percent or more.

- Consider dropping collision and/or comprehensive coverage on older cars.

- Buy a "low profile" car. Cars that are expensive to repair have higher insurance costs.

- Take advantage of low-mileage discounts. Some companies offer discounts to motorists who drive fewer than a set number of miles a year.

- Find out about discounts for air bags, antilock brakes, daytime running lights. There are also safe-driver discounts, such as for no accidents in three years or no moving violations in recent years.

- Maintain good credit. Depending on your state, your credit score may influence your insurance rate.

make a living as a dishonest used car dealer. (Danny DeVito played Matilda's father in the movie. He gleefully cheats his customers by spinning back odometers, putting sawdust in engines, and tapping into other tricks of the trade to con customers into buying clunkers for a hefty price.) While there are still bad used car dealers in every community, your choices are much improved. For one thing, cars are more durable and the overall quality is higher. For another, more dealers have gotten into the business and the competition has upgraded the whole process.

The best place to buy a used car remains from a friend or acquaintance. You know their driving habits, and you'll get an honest answer about how the car has been treated. Both of you should come out ahead financially, too. You aren't paying a middleman to broker the deal. If you don't know someone with a decent car for sale, I'd check out the new car dealers in your area. Many of them have moved into the used car business in a big way, especially with formerly leased cars. Dealers will often offer extended warranties on used cars. The used car superstores are a competitive force that offers buyers choice, no-haggle pricing, and warranties.

Of course, a used car to some extent is damaged goods by definition. You will inherit someone else's problems. The previous owner may have had a lead foot. The owner might have been careless in changing the oil and other fluids. Problems could lurk in the fuel line, the brakes, and transmission. Taking a used car that intrigues you to a mechanic you trust is critical to protecting yourself from buying a future of automotive repair bills. If you've done your homework well, a used car will save you a lot of money.

Budget

A budget is simply a way to seize control over financial chaos. It helps us stop spending more than we earn. We know we're wasting money, but we're not sure on what. The payoff from a budget is that you end up spending your money where you want and save for what you would like to do. For a relatively small investment in time and effort up front, a budget has the potential to generate a lifetime of good financial habits.

What goes into a budget? Everything. The classic budget template converts expenses into monthly numbers. For example, if you pay $600 annually for life insurance, divide that figure by 12 to get $50. Similarly, if you spend $150 a week on food, multiply it by 4 to get $600. A number of excellent budget templates are on the Web. For instance, Mint.com offers an easy online budgeting tool. The Consumer Credit Counseling Service of San Francisco (www.cccssf.org) has a comprehensive budget planner you can print out.

Here's the basic outline of the exercise. It starts with the essential monthly expenditures: housing, food, insurance, medical care, transportation, child care, miscellaneous (such as laundry, pet care, and union dues), income taxes, and savings. You add it all up. Then you start putting down the monthly discretionary expenses: personal (beauty salon, cosmetics, and the like), entertainment (cable TV, movie, sports, and so on), and miscellaneous (gifts, booze, Internet service, etc.). Next comes all your unsecured debt, namely credit cards. That's followed by your total monthly income and your net income. You're now in a position to calculate the bottom line: i.e., your monthly net income minus your total monthly expenses.

It's important to come up with a system that's comfortable for you. The good news is that technology makes it easier than ever to budget. Several excellent computer programs exist for data management. The best-known product is by Quicken. It is comprehensive, although the information may be more than you need. Quicken has so many features that it's a real commitment to learn the program. A good technique if you're disciplined is to put everything on a credit card, then download it into the computer. It works only if you pay the bill off in full at month's end. If your money problem is debt, I don't recommend this approach.

The new generation of online services for budgeting is good. For example, Mint.com will aggregate all your credit card, savings, investment, mortgage, auto-loan, and other financial data. You mine the information to see where your money is going. The program also has built-in guides for attacking your most expensive debts first. Mint is a monitoring tool (you can only read the data, you can't transfer money around) that facilitates budgeting. The big caveat to Mint and a number of similar pro-

grams is that you give out your user name and password to your financial
accounts to access the data. Some competing programs offer a way to use
their program without divulging your password. For example, Wesabe
.com lets you export and upload the financial information yourself. It's a
lot more cumbersome, but some customers like the extra layer of protection. The Web-based budgeting-tool sites keep getting better, too. Many
banks, credit unions, and other financial institutions offer online budgeting programs to their customers.

It's fine if you prefer monitoring spending with an old-fashioned
notebook and pencil, making simple additions and subtractions on a
cheap calculator. It's more than adequate in most circumstances.

Budgeting is a tool, not a goal. You don't need to devote a lot of time to
this. You shouldn't have to track your spending data over the years unless
you want to or have a good reason for making the effort. For a relatively
small investment in time and effort up front, a budget transforms itself
into a lifetime of good financial habits. At that point, ballpark figures and
estimates suffice for most people. "Do you really need to be tracking all
spending on a monthly basis?" asks Eric Tyson, the author of a number of
bestselling personal-finance books. "Because if you set a specific savings
goal like 'we're going to save 10% of our income or 8% of our income
each month' and you're able to do that, then my feeling is who cares
where it goes after you have accomplished that savings."

Incentives Matter

We know it's hard to stick with a budget in the early stages. Our intentions are good, but life interferes and old habits reemerge. The next
thing you know, you're back in the hole, saving too little and spending
too much. It's a bit like those New Year's resolutions about diet and exercise, isn't it?

First, cut yourself some slack. Don't try to do everything at once. It's a
journey, not a destination. Second, engage with your community. Talk
about what you're trying to do with friends when you get together at a

coffee shop and on social-media Web sites such as Facebook and My-Space. We all feel an obligation to live up to what we say with friends. You can give them status updates, and they'll offer encouragement and share their tales of budgeting goals.

You can tap into the power of money as a commitment strategy. That's what economist Peter Orszag does. He's an economist and director of the White House's Office of Management and Budget. In an interview on National Public Radio, he mentioned that he tries to use economic insights not only as a government official but in his private life. He's a marathon runner, and to keep motivated he built a financial penalty into his training regimen. "If I didn't achieve what I wanted to, a very large contribution would automatically come out of my credit card and go to a charity that I very much didn't support," says Orszag. "So that was a very strong motivation, as I was running through mile fifteen or sixteen or whatever it was, to remind myself that I really didn't want to give the satisfaction to that charity for the contribution." He didn't name the charity. But I like the idea.

It's a technique economist Richard McKenzie would endorse. The University of California at Irvine professor came up with his own Economist Weight-Loss Incentive Plan. McKenzie described the motivation for his "dieting for dollars" approach in an article in the *Wall Street Journal*: "I had been trying to lose 10 pounds for what seemed like a decade. I had lost about 378 pounds during my struggle, only to remain nine pounds short of my target weight." His solution? He did a deal with a friend. He would pay her $500 if he hadn't lost nine pounds in ten weeks. The contract spelled out that the friend had to spend the money on herself. The signing of the contract was witnessed. It worked. He lost fourteen pounds by the end of the ten weeks.

The key is a public commitment. Trained economists may be more sensitive to financial incentives than the normal person. For others, the desire not to let down their friends and earn their admiration is incentive enough to help exercise self-control.

By now, you're aware I also believe that sustainability is a motivating force. The impact of sustainability ideas encouraging us to be more frugal, to be conscious consumers and mindful investors shouldn't be underestimated.

Much of the money you free up by budgeting goes into savings. You borrow less, if at all. Your household finances are more secure. But there's another aspect of creating a margin of safety that I want to emphasize: Your insurance backstop and your estate plan. Let's start with insurance, specifically life insurance.

Life Insurance Is Critical

There is only one reason to buy life insurance: to financially protect your loved ones from your untimely death. Indeed, once your kids have left home and are building their own lives you probably won't need much life insurance—if any. How much life insurance should you own? Industry experts typically recommend a family with two children consider purchasing life insurance worth six to eight times family income. It's a sensible starting point for asking lots of questions. The sum may be larger if your spouse doesn't have a full-time paying job. It affects how much insurance you'll want if you plan on sending your kids to expensive private colleges or cheaper public universities. Even married folks without children should look at life insurance. For instance, should each of you carry enough insurance so if one of you dies the other doesn't have to worry about money for a period of time? The survivor can take a year or more—you decide—to deal with their grief, without worrying about earning an income, paying down debts, or draining the savings account.

What type of life insurance should you buy? There are two basic kinds. The first is "term" life insurance. It's a pure death benefit. Term insurance is relatively cheap, but the cost of a policy goes up as you age. Term insurance is a simple product that allows for competitive comparison-shopping for the best mix of price and coverage. You'll want a low-cost, plain-vanilla policy from a blue chip, financially strong life insurance company. Term insurance is ideal for most families, especially since there are so many other demands on your money.

The other major category is called "permanent" or "cash value" insurance. It always comes with a tax-sheltered savings component as well as a life insurance policy. There are all kinds of cash value policies, including whole-life, universal-life, variable-life, and variable-universal life. Depending on the type of cash value policy, the insurance company may invest the savings for you or you can choose from a menu of mutual funds offered by the insurer. The premium may be stable for the life of the policy or you may vary your payments. Cash value policies are expensive compared to term. Commission costs are high, the policies' inner workings are often obscure, and premiums are costly.

That said, cash value insurance can be a smart buy. I think it's an attractive option for those people who still have money left over after contributing the maximum into retirement savings plans and adding to their already hefty savings accounts. In that case, a cash value policy offers another way to save and protect your family against your untimely death. You can get at the cash value in a permanent policy by borrowing against it. If you think a cash value policy is the way to go, take your time, shop around, and get competitive bids. Once again, only do business with highly rated companies. I would lean toward the simpler, plain-vanilla cash value policies and steer clear of fancy twists and turns. They're expensive and they disappoint.

For most people, the better savings strategy is to buy term and invest the difference. In other words, let's say the monthly premium on a whole life policy is $150 and a term policy $30. You buy the term life insurance coverage and invest the $120 on your own into a savings account or mutual fund. It's a classic margin-of-safety approach.

Don't Forget Disability Insurance

It's really paycheck protection or, more accurately, partial paycheck protection. Disability insurance replaces a portion of your income if you can't work because of an illness or injury. According to the Life and

Health Insurance Foundation for Education, an industry trade group, about one in five Americans will become disabled for one year or more before reaching age sixty-five.

Many employees get disability insurance through work. If you're self-employed you'll need to find an individual disability policy. A policy will typically replace about 60 percent of your income. There are a couple of features to emphasize. Make sure the policy covers your occupation. If you should become disabled, the benefit should protect you against inflation. It should also be a "noncancelable" and "guaranteed renewable" policy. With this type of policy the insurance company can't change your premiums or cancel your coverage as long as you make your payments on time.

A Health Insurance Check-up

The wild card in all financial planning is health insurance. Our broken-down health insurance system leaves far too many people with inadequate coverage or uninsured. Many people are vulnerable to large out-of-pocket expenses. The long-term forecasts are worrisome. Paul Fronstin of the Employee Benefits Research Institute estimated that a fifty-five-year-old couple in 2006 planning to retire at age sixty-five would need to accumulate $400,000 during the next ten years to afford what Medicare doesn't cover through age ninety. "Thus saving for retirement may ultimately be less about the golf condo at Hilton Head and more about being able to afford wheelchair lifts, private nurses, and a high-quality nursing home," says Jonathan Skinner, economist at Dartmouth College, in "Are You Sure You're Saving Enough for Retirement?"

It's numbers like these that convince me that the push toward major health care reform will continue in coming years. The competitive pressure from the global economy is forcing society and legislators to embrace health insurance policies that will improve the economic security and financial welfare of millions of working- and middle-class Americans. We'll continue to make strides toward universal health care coverage, as

momentous a public policy change for the average worker and family as
the creation of Social Security in 1935 and Medicare in 1965.

That said, my hope is that you work for a company that offers a
health insurance plan. You may be upset at rising premium payments
and shrunken coverage, but there is still nothing better than employer-
provided health insurance for working-age families. The self-employed
have a number of options, such as buying into a group health plan
through a trade organization, community group, professional association, or some other alliance. Some health maintenance organizations
will sell to individuals, as will the Blue Cross/Blue Shield plans.

However, the most intriguing option for the self-employed is Health
Savings Accounts or HSAs. An HSA plan comes in two parts. First, you
must buy a health insurance policy with a high deductible. Then you
open an HSA, a tax-sheltered account much like an individual retirement account. The account is funded with pretax contributions and the
money is sheltered from taxes. The maximum contribution that can
be made to an HSA in 2010 for employees with single coverage is $3,050.
The contribution for family coverage is $6,150. These figures are ad-
justed yearly.

Withdrawals from the account are tax-free so long as the money goes
toward qualified medical expenses, which include everything from acu-
puncture to organ transplants to quit-smoking programs. The money is
usually parked in a bank-like account, and beneficiaries of the plan receive a checkbook or debit card for paying their medical bills.

The idea behind the high-deductible/HSA plans is this: Catastrophic
coverage prevents serious medical illness from financially crippling
an individual or family. HSAs are complex and many consumers rebel
against paying several thousand dollars out-of-pocket, even if it is with
tax-free money. You need to have the cash to fund the HSA. These plans
are inhospitable for anyone with preexisting conditions such as cancer
or diabetes. Still, despite its drawbacks for the self-employed it's one of
the better options available at the moment.

The case for long-term care insurance is compelling. A year in a nursing home runs an average of some $50,000. It can easily run $30,000 or more a year to live in an assisted living center with professional care. Home care is even more costly. Yet Medicare and regular health insurance policies don't cover these astronomical costs.

Problem is, the case for buying long-term care insurance isn't compelling. It's a complicated, expensive product. The Kaiser Family Foundation tried to calculate whether long-term care insurance was a practical financial product for middle-class families. The study's first pass on the data suggested that three out of four married couples (with the head of household between ages thirty-five and fifty-nine) could theoretically afford LTCI. Premiums are much more affordable when younger. Yet on a closer look, only one in five is well covered in other key areas, like saving for retirement, life insurance, health insurance, and disability insurance. Those other investments should take precedence.

As for older people, premiums are so steep that it's much harder to afford comprehensive coverage. The more affordable pared-down products that are on the market don't really offer meaningful protection. It's a product worth investigating, but I'd be skeptical. Shopping for LTCI is an educational process. It's a case where most people will need an expert to help them evaluate policies, pricing, and their needs. In the end, I think the answer in many cases will be it isn't worth the cost.

Estate Planning

Ah, estate planning. Sounds fancy, doesn't it? Well, it isn't. Estate planning is about limiting risk and bringing order to your finances. Now, I'm not going to worry about estate taxes. It's an issue for a small number of multimillionaires and if it's a concern for you, you'll already have financial advisers on your payroll. No, I want to focus on something far more mundane and important: a will.

A will is simply written instructions, prepared according to legal rules, that say how your property is to be distributed at death. A will is

---

A trust is a legal entity created by a property owner that protects and distributes the property according to the owner's wishes. One reason more people are turning to trusts is that the estate avoids probate, and probate has a terrible reputation. A probate court administers a person's will. It's the legal process of settling an estate and your will becomes a public document. But probate is not as bad as it's often alleged. And in far too many cases trusts are sold to people who really don't need them. There are many different types of trusts. They can be complex. Here are a couple of questions to ask if you're wondering if a trust should be in your future.

- Are any of your beneficiaries physically or mentally handicapped?

- Do you or your beneficiaries need protection from creditors?

- Is there a relative you don't want to include as a beneficiary?

- Is there a business, property, or a financial portfolio that needs professional management?

- Do you want to control how your estate is used after your death?

- Do you want to restrict access to your estate by your heirs until they reach a certain age?

> • Is there substantial property in several states?
>
> • Do you want to keep prying eyes away from your financial affairs?
>
> If the answer is yes to these questions (or some of them) I would talk to an estate lawyer. Come with lots of questions and a skeptical frame of mind.

vital for protecting the financial interests of your children. It's critical to think about who you want to raise your children if you and your spouse die or if you are a single parent. It's increasingly common to designate one person to raise your children and another person, with better money skills, to take care of the finances. A will is not a once-in-a-lifetime document. People usually outgrow their initial wills as their circumstances change.

You should also consider who you want to carry out your wishes should you become severely ill or incompetent. The three most common documents that deal with this are a power of attorney for financial issues, a power of attorney for health care, and a living will. The latter lays out your wishes about life-prolonging health care procedures.

Everyone needs a will. And this is a case where I think it pays to hire a lawyer that specializes in wills. Yes, the software and Internet do-it-yourself wills are decent products, but this is an area where the cliché is true—don't be penny-wise and pound-foolish.

CHAPTER 6

Borrow Wisely

*Go confidently in the direction of your dreams. Live the life
you have imagined.*

—Henry David Thoreau

You don't want to end up in the black glass skyscraper in the heart of
downtown Memphis, Tennessee. It's popularly known as the Bankruptcy
Building. It's where people in Memphis who have too much debt end up.

The eleventh floor is crowded with lawyers, paralegals, and bankrupt
folks. Four U.S. trustees appointed by the federal government try to re-
solve cases so that they don't end up before a bankruptcy judge two
floors down. An attorney strolls by and says, "Memphis is known for the
blues, Beale Street, barbecue, and bankruptcy!"

This bankruptcy "court" isn't majestic or awe-inspiring like a criminal
court. It has no black-robed judges, dark-paneled walls, let alone a jury
box or a judge's raised podium. No, the impression is more of a clean
bus-terminal waiting room. The rows of plastic chairs are gray. The walls
are painted a different shade of gray. The carpet is dull green. In small
pockets throughout the room borrowers huddle with their attorneys.

In a side room sits George Stevenson, a U.S. trustee. The sixty-plus-
year-old is a trim former marine with close-cropped white hair. He wears
black slacks and a yellow polo shirt. He sits in front of a computer. At his

elbow are a middle-aged woman and her attorney. "Ah, this is a motion to surrender the house you've been living in?" asks Stevenson.

"Yes, sir," the woman replies.

"And you're going to let that go. Tell us why?"

"My husband's on drugs. He abandoned me. I left the house. I've been paying with garnisheed wages—seven hundred dollars plus rent. Here are the keys! I can't afford to maintain a house."

Seconds later, her case is disposed. A young woman in a sweat suit and her lawyer are next.

"You've been having trouble making your plan payments," says Stevenson.

"Laid off from my job," the young woman says.

"When will you get back to work?"

"Soon, hopefully. I have been looking but haven't found anything yet."

"Think you might if we gave you a little more time?" Stevenson wonders.

"Yes."

It's like a smoothly operating assembly line. Everyone is treated with respect. The courtly Stevenson listens to story after story. A woman with a failing small drapery business. A marriage gone south along with finances.

Sometimes, trouble comes from the ominous but all-too-common combination of youth and financial ignorance. That's the story of Maria. When radio producer Sasha Aslanian and I met her, she was a twenty-nine-year-old single mother of four, easily mistaken for a college student with her slender frame and youthful face. LUSCIOUS was tattooed in cursive on the side of her neck. She said she moved out of her parents' home in Memphis at age nineteen and wasn't careful about what loan agreements she signed. "Your credit's like your word," she said. "And nobody explained that to me."

She worked as a customer-service rep making $10 an hour. She owed an amount equal to her annual wages—about $21,000—mostly for some student loans, back rent, and costly furniture-rental payments. Creditors were hounding her for payment. "It's very depressing when all you can think about is trying to keep your head above water," she said.

Filing for bankruptcy relieves a household of an onerous debt burden. It's a chance to start over in your financial life. But not all debts can be forgiven in bankruptcy. Among the main debts that can't be discharged under most circumstances are:

Student loans

Child Support and Alimony

Debts you owe from a divorce decree or settlement

Consumer debts for luxury goods or services incurred in the months leading up to bankruptcy

Fines and penalties imposed for violating the law, like criminal fines and court-ordered repayments

Debts or judgments that arose from a fraudulent or illegal act, like causing injury or death as a drunk driver

Income taxes from recent years

Maria was filing personal bankruptcy for relief from her bills. She dreamed of finishing college, maybe starting her own beauty salon. "I hope bankruptcy will give me a fresh start so I can go about owning my own home for me and my children," she said.

Many of the folks we met in and around the Bankruptcy Building had been preyed upon by high-cost, high-fee lenders in poorer neighborhoods. Still, the debt problem isn't confined to low-income folks. Credit card debts, mortgage debt, home-equity loans, car loans, and student loans have overwhelmed millions of homeowners in tony suburbs and better-off blue-collar neighborhoods, brand-new exurbs, and downtown condos. Families had little financial margin against a setback, such as a medical illness, a job loss, or a divorce.

Marion Chase Pacheco was unlucky three times over. She lost her job, went through a divorce, and suffered from a major illness. When I met her, she was living in a small apartment in New Rochelle, on the outskirts of New York City. In her midfifties, her three children were all grown-up, and she was happy as could be about a new granddaughter. She had a bad back that started when a truck hit her in college. She'd been a teacher, but her back troubles convinced her to pursue a new career—one she could do from a wheelchair if necessary: the law. She and her husband, a doctor, were living in Syracuse, New York. She went to Syracuse Law School at age forty-seven and passed her bar exam when she was fifty. The price tag for her law degree was $60,000 in student loans. She and her husband had already taken on debt to send their children to private colleges.

Problem is, she didn't make much as a lawyer. When she and her husband divorced, there was nothing to split but debt. Her financial problems started to mount. She moved down to New Rochelle after she met a new partner, thinking there'd be better job prospects for a lawyer in the Big Apple. But there weren't. "Who wants to hire a lawyer who is fifty-six?" she asked. "Nobody around here anyway."

To top it off, Marion was deep in hock for medical bills related to her back. She was so broke she ended up representing herself in court. Of course, bankruptcy didn't clear up all of Marion's debt problems. By law, bankruptcy can't get rid of her student loans, which total $100,000 for herself and her kids. Marion did find some work as a substitute teacher, despite her bad back. But she has no retirement savings. She calculates it will take her until she's ninety years old to pay back her law school loans. Eventually, she moved to South Carolina to be closer to her kids, who settled in the Palmetto State several years earlier.

Borrow with a Margin of Safety

Living debt-free is wonderful. But sometimes borrowing is a savvy move. The key to avoiding the debt trap is borrowing with a margin of safety. That's what Sara and her husband did. They live in Golden Valley, Minnesota, and they had managed to pay off all of their debts except for their mortgage. They'd achieved their debt goal despite Sara's being laid off twice in the previous eighteen months. She had just got a new job when she e-mailed me, "We desperately need a new car. We could pay for it with cash from liquid funds, or we could finance it very reasonably from a credit union or USAA [an insurance company]. Would it be good for us to have some non-home-related debt with regular payments (our credit score should already be good because we always pay on time)? Or, should we aim to have as little debt as possible and pay cash? We do have reserves in case of unemployment."

They were responsible borrowers. Borrowing to buy a car wasn't a recipe for future financial problems. They were rightly reluctant to take on debt—my normal advice is to pay cash. Yet in their case, a loan made sense. At the time, businesses were laying off workers rapidly and any economic relief seemed far off. Savings are critical in all seasons, but especially in an environment like that. By borrowing—using Other People's Money—she and her husband got the car they needed and maintained their financial flexibility. Their pot of emergency savings remained full, and they were committed to add to it. They could—and should—pay off the loan once they have a better sense of their job security.

Similarly, Carl from Alameda, California, got in touch with me by e-mail from Singapore, where he was working on a contract job. "Given today's low returns on money market accounts and CDs, is now a good time to pay off one's mortgage?" he asked. "I am about halfway through my 15-year, 4.875%, fixed-rate mortgage and plan to keep the house. The mortgage balance is $110,000. I have been 'maxing out' my 401(k) for the last 18 years and am fortunate enough to work for a company that will provide a defined-benefit pension. I have low expenses, no debt other than this mortgage, and an income that allows me to save several thousand after-tax dollars each month. I have $250,000, after tax, in a money market account—more than enough for emergencies. I am thinking of using $110,000 of my after-tax cash to pay off my mortgage. Given the low returns on money market accounts and CDs, the argument for using extra cash to pay off debt, including mortgage debt, seems to warrant greater merit, right?"

In the heart of every homeowner burns an intense desire to say good-bye to the bank for the last time and own a home free and clear. It's a wonderful moment, and if you have the money, there's nothing wrong with paying off the mortgage to live debt-free. Yet I'm wary of vastly accelerating mortgage payments for many people. It all has to do with a margin of safety.

For one thing, you're putting most of your financial eggs in one basket—a home. Your financial health is now dependent on how that asset performs in coming years. You're very exposed to the local economy and job market. That's why I prefer that most people focus on building up a well-diversified portfolio of cash, stocks, and bonds, and not just in retirement savings accounts. You want to have money you can tap without paying the 10 percent penalty you fork out if you access your retirement account under the age of 59½. Over time, a home should shrink as a percentage of your net worth. If paying off your mortgage drains your savings or retirement funds, it will increase your vulnerability.

However, Carl was in a good financial position. He had a big emergency fund, after-tax savings, and he was fully funding his retirement savings plan at work. He had a company pension, too, and no other debt other than his mortgage. He was well diversified, so he would not be concentrating his net worth into one asset. Why not be debt-free? It was a smart financial move.

Foolish Debt and Wise Debt

Let's take another journey back in financial history. The U.S. economy expanded rapidly during the nineteenth century, and the Victorian era was characterized by entrepreneurial opportunity and everyday optimism. Reflecting society's increasing wealth, the standard money advice in books and magazines shifted from "debt is bad" to "debt can be good, sometimes."

A popular distinction was drawn between "consumptive debt" and "productive credit." It's really a variation on the distinction between needs and wants. The ominous-sounding "consumptive" debt included borrowing for everything from clothes to entertainment. Historian Lendol Calder notes, "Consumption signified the wasting disease of tuberculosis. This loathsome association accounts for the stock portrayals of consumptive debtors in the money ethic literature: shivering youths who pawned overcoats to pay gambling debt; sallow New York dandies with showy chains on their vest . . . Borrowing money for 'gratifications of the moment' was the only kind of debt strictly forbidden by the money ethic."

In sharp contrast, productive credit was borrowing money to make money. Even using the word *credit* rather than *debt* signaled a more positive act. *Credit* derives from the Latin word for "believe" or "trust," while *debt* in Latin is "to owe." Over time the examples of productive credit expanded from borrowing to start a business or own land to include loans for buying a home, reapers, sewing machines, and pianos, according to Calder.

In the installment-borrowing revolution of the 1920s, the phrase *consumptive debt* fell out of favor. It was transformed into the benign *consumer credit*, a term that aligned consumer borrowing with the positive vision of productive credit. The key thinker behind that transformation was economist E. R. A. Seligman, author of the groundbreaking *Economics of Installment Selling.* The main force in the consumer-borrowing business was John Jakob Raskob, head of General Motors Acceptance Corporation, the giant automaker's lending subsidiary.

Still, the idea of bad debt (consumptive debt) and good debt (productive credit) was never really abandoned. It's a worthwhile distinction even as it has evolved over the decades. Good debt offers a rate of return. It's an investment in our future. A home mortgage is a classic case of good debt. Another example is borrowing to pay for a college education.

Conversely, bad debt is frivolous. It's spending weekends at the mall and taking on credit card debt. It's buying a $4,000 watch on credit when you earn $28,000 a year. A couple of years ago, we wandered the streets and asked people, "What's the most ridiculous thing you've ever charged?" Among the answers were "The silliest thing I ever did with a credit card is I got a cash advance to pay my other credit card." "Silliest? Oh, chocolates, emery boards, something really silly." "A soda. For a dollar." "Just about everything I charge is ridiculous."

The terms I prefer are *wise debt* and *foolish debt*. I've done both, far too much of the latter, and not enough of the former. The difference isn't the type of debt, but the margin of safety.

Look at credit cards for an illustration. A former boss of mine was fond of saying that for many people personal finance meant getting out of credit card debt. Sadly, he was right. Yet another friend puts everything on his credit card every month, from groceries to gas. He pays off the bill in full at the end of the month. He could pay cash for what he puts on the card. He doesn't because over the years he's accumulated plenty of points for cheap airfares to visit his adult children or take a vacation and stay at luxury hotels at cut-rate prices. He always had a margin of safety—the cash on hand—and the discipline to pay the bill. He used credit cards to accomplish other goals at a cheap price. That's a wise use of debt.

A mortgage can be foolish debt. That's the case with Seth and Joanna Goslin. They told their story to *Marketplace Money* host Tess Vigeland in spring 2008. Three years earlier they bought for $193,000 a twelve-hundred-square-foot condo in Elk Grove, California. Joanna was a stay-at-home mom raising their two young daughters. Seth was a mortgage broker. Their initial home loan was a 2/28 adjustable rate mortgage (ARM). The mortgage interest rate was fixed for the first two years, then adjusted afterward depending on market conditions for the next twenty-eight years. The Goslins financed 100 percent of the purchase price—no down payment. To lower their monthly mortgage bill they refinanced into an even riskier mortgage, an "option" ARM. With an option ARM, borrowers can choose to make payments that don't cover the interest on the loan. Problem is, those lower payments balloon the mortgage tab over time. "I mean, we understood that it was a risk, but we sort of just assumed that it would kind of work out," Joanna said.

The property appreciated at first by about 10 percent. But Joanna got pregnant. Seth lost his job. Real estate prices fell. In 2008 the same condo model as theirs in the next building was priced at $95,000—less than half of what they paid. They ended up losing the condo in foreclosure and eventually declared bankruptcy. Seth and Joanna didn't have a sufficient margin of safety.

So, to deliberately repeat myself, risk matters: If you borrow with a margin of safety and something goes wrong in your life, you will feel financial pressure and suffer money anxiety. Who doesn't? But you'll have resources to draw on to get you through the turmoil. The financial outcome can be catastrophic if you borrow, believe that everything will work out fine, and don't protect against the consequences of being wrong. It's why being debt free is the goal.

I hear it all the time: People don't want to get rid of their mortgage because they don't want to lose the mortgage interest deduction. My response? Get rid of the mortgage.

The advantages of the mortgage interest deduction are greatly exaggerated. It's a nice benefit, but it's far from a financial windfall. For one thing, most couples living outside the most expensive metropolitan areas or the more exclusive neighborhoods around the country can do almost as well by simply taking advantage of the standard deduction. Put somewhat differently, the mortgage interest deduction becomes valuable the higher your income and the more expensive your home. But for most people it isn't that big a deal. For another, the mortgage interest deduction seems to encourage people to buy a bigger home than they need, and that's a mistake. Most importantly, the debt needs to be repaid and the interest payments add up over time swamping the effect of a tax deduction.

Don't let taxes determine your borrowing and investment strategy. It's the underlying economics of your household finances that matter. Only then take taxes into consideration.

Leaving the Debt Trap Behind

Let's begin with getting rid of debts since that is what so many people are trying to do. Almost all of us are anxious when we run into debt trouble. We're juggling bills, our income is stretched, and interest charges are eroding our finances. Right when we're near the point of eliminating our debt, we get hit with an unexpected bill, such as a major car repair or the IRS asking for payment on a miscalculated tax. (I'm speaking from experience.) The setback is demoralizing.

I wish I could say there's a magic formula for quickly eliminating debt and reducing stress. There isn't. That said, there's no reason for despair. Some time-tested solutions work. People reduce and eliminate their debt burdens all the time. It requires several steps and trade-offs—and patience, lots of patience.

- Figure out how much you really owe.

- Make debt reduction a priority. Other financial demands or desires go on the back burner.

- Create a budget, and siphon the savings toward debt.

- Have a plan that lays out which debts to tackle first, second, third, and so on.

- Remember, small steps add up over time.

- Don't take on any new loans.

- The goal is to get out of debt in one to five years (not including your primary mortgage and student loans).

- Keep the big picture in mind: less stress, better finances, and a happier life.

For most people, the consumer debts that push them toward the financial precipice are credit cards and retail cards, home-equity loans and lines of credit, and vehicle loans. I'm going to focus on expensive credit cards for my examples. But the same tactics and strategies apply if your menu of debts includes auto loans, home-equity debts, mortgages, and student loans. (There is unusual flexibility with federal student loans.)

Remember the concept of compound interest? It's the saver's friend. It's the borrower's enemy. For instance, you're carrying a balance of $10,000 at an interest rate of 18.9 percent. You're only paying the minimum each month. It would take you fifty-three years and $34,336 in interest charges to pay off the debt, according to the Federal Reserve's Credit Card Calculator at federalreserve.gov/creditcardcalculator. Those are scary numbers.

Let's look again at the $10,000 credit card debt at an 18.9 percent rate. This time we increase the initial payment to $250. Now, here's the real trick: You keep sending in $250 a month even though the required minimum payment will shrink with time. You ignore that lower minimum

Common warning signs that you're in credit card trouble:

Are your credit card balances mounting despite your best efforts to pay down your debt?

Do you find yourself making the minimum payment on this month's bill, last month's bill, and so on?

Are you tapping into one of your credit cards to pay off another credit card debt?

Are you having trouble meeting the minimum payment?

Are you using your credit cards to pay for food, utilities, and other essentials even as your old bills pile up in a desk drawer?

charge. By maintaining a $250-a-month payment you will eliminate the debt in five years and fork over $5,907 in interest charges. That's not great, but it's a lot better than more than a half century and over $34,000 in interest. Send in a consistent $300 a month and the debt is gone in four years and $4,292 in interest; a $350 monthly payment, it's three years and $3,391 in interest; and so on. Again, small steps add up. Many

Don't borrow on your home equity to pay down more expensive debts such as credit cards. A home-equity loan (also called a second mortgage) is a lump sum of money. You pay it back regularly over time, just like a mortgage. A home-equity line of credit allows you to write a check (or use a special credit card) whenever you need to borrow against the equity in your home. The interest rate is typically fixed with a home-equity loan, and the rate fluctuates with a home-equity line of credit. In both cases the equity in your home acts as collateral.

In general, a fixed-rate home-equity loan is tailor-made for major remodeling projects, such as a new kitchen or bathroom. The variable-rate home-equity line of credit is better for smaller projects that are accomplished over a longer period of time. The money borrowed against the equity in your home should go toward improving the value of your home and your enjoyment of it. It shouldn't be used to pay down other debts.

Yes, the interest rate on a home-equity loan or a home-equity line of credit is lower than credit card charges. You get to deduct the interest on the home-equity loan and credit lines. But it's a risky strategy. You have put your house at risk. If you miss credit card payments, the credit card company can't go after your house. But if you miss home-equity loan or line-of-credit payments, foreclosure is a genuine risk.

credit unions, banks, and mutual-fund companies offer calculators where you can play with the numbers. I also like the debt calculators at dinkytown.net and those suggested at choosetosave.org.

How should you handle more than one card with different balances and interest rates? For instance, perhaps your $10,000 in debt is composed of $5,000 with a 21 percent interest rate, $3,000 at 17 percent, and $2,000 at 14 percent. You can try a debt roll-up, a technique I learned from Gerri Detweiler, a longtime consumer advocate and president of Ultimate Credit Solutions Inc. The basic idea is to pay the minimum on all your debts except the highest-rate one. That's where you target the extra savings you're eking out with a budget. Eventually that debt is gone. You attack the highest-rate debt that remains, paying the minimum on the others, until all the loans are paid off. In the $10,000 total-debt example, you'd pay the minimum on the $3,000 and the $2,000 credit cards. Throw as much as possible at the $5,000 debt. When it's paid off, you would meet the minimum on the $2,000 card and put the extra money into the $3,000 debt. It's another strategy that builds momentum with the passage of time.

The mathematics of finance dictates it's usually best to attack the highest-rate debt first. It's your most expensive borrowing. However, many of us need a psychological boost when we're trying to stick to a debt-repayment plan. We need a sense of accomplishment to keep going, concrete evidence that our efforts are worth it. In that case, attack your smallest bill first and eliminate it as fast as possible. Congratulations. Now, go after the next smallest debt.

A number of other steps could help if they lower the interest rate on your debt. For instance, consolidation loans offer the convenience of one payment, and if it cuts your rate, it can be a savvy move. Problem is, the price tag of convenience is usually too high. Consolidating your loans could end up costing you more, not less, especially if the lender lengthens the terms of your loan and charges various fees. It's also worth trying to renegotiate rates with lenders. It never hurts to ask. However, steer clear of the outfits that advertise on the radio and cable saying

Freeze the credit card

Put the credit card away when you're eliminating debt. One technique is to store the card in the freezer. That's right, place the credit card in a container of water and stick it in the freezer. You have to wait for it to thaw before you can use it again. It gives you time to think whether you really want to use it. Yes, the card will work once it's thawed.

they'll renegotiate your debts—for a hefty fee, of course. Too many of these companies take advantage of people already down on their luck. It's too difficult to figure out which ones are legitimate and which ones aren't.

In Deep Debt Trouble

What if you're truly overwhelmed by debt? You've run some numbers and you can't see how you'll emerge from your financial hole. Don't despair. Get professional help. Now, the credit-counseling industry is ripe with fraud, malfeasance, and fly-by-night operators. That's why I would check out a branch of the National Foundation for Credit Counseling (NFCC), founded in 1951. It's the biggest and oldest national nonprofit credit-counseling service, with branches all over the country. Many of its members offer Internet, phone, and in-person counseling. The fees range from zero to $30. The quality of the service can vary, but it's a legitimate organization and a good place to start. The United Way and a number of churches also offer referrals and services. Unions typically strike deals with debt-reduction outfits to get their members access to credit counseling.

When you go to a credit-counseling service, the counselor will go over your financial situation. The counselor and you come up with a monthly

Resources for troubled debtors

Nolo.com has been around since 1971, and the company's lawyers offer affordable, plainly written books, forms, and software on a wide range of legal and financial issues, including debt and bankruptcy. Nolo is constantly updating its information. I've worked with their experts for years, and I'm always impressed with the quality of their knowledge and their passion to help consumers.

Reduce Debt, Reduce Stress by Gerri Detweiler, Nancy Castleman, and Marc Eisenson (Good Advice Press, 2009). These three veterans of the getting-out-of-consumer-debt movement really know their stuff. They offer practical information on all aspects of escaping debt.

The National Foundation for Credit Counseling is at nfcc.org. The toll-free number is 1-800-388-2227. Don't be embarrassed. Don't be shy. The debt counselors have seen everything. They will design a debt-reduction plan with you.

National Association of Consumer Bankruptcy Attorneys is at nacba.org. The Web site of the American Bankruptcy Institute is abiworld.org. If you need to look for a bankruptcy lawyer, you can start at either place.

spending plan that deals with your living expenses and payments to creditors. In essence, the counselor brings order out of the chaos with a budget. Sometimes, the combination of a consultation and practical advice is all a stressed-out borrower needs. For others, however, it may be a smart move to set up a debt-repayment plan with the service. In essence, you deposit money each month into an account at the credit-counseling agency. It takes the money to pay creditors along the lines of your repayment plan developed by you and the counselor. The agency lobbies creditors to try to get better loan terms for you, such as reducing the amount you owe or at least reducing the interest charges and fees. The agency will negotiate to stop collection actions against you. However, if a creditor won't participate in the debt-repayment plan, you have to pay that bill off separately.

Sometimes, with so much debt relative to income, bankruptcy is the only way out. It's a drastic step, a last resort, but it's also a way to get a fresh start, a second chance. You'll want to consult with an attorney to explore your options and to ensure that filing for financial relief with the courts will improve your situation.

The two main types of personal bankruptcy are Chapter 7 and Chapter 13. Chapter 7 bankruptcy lets you get rid of unsecured debts, such as medical bills and credit cards. It's also called "liquidation" bankruptcy. It's a relatively simple process. A trustee appointed by the court gathers together and sells all your assets, with the exception of your exempt property. You're allowed to keep the exempt property, which usually includes the equity in your home, the cash value of your insurance policies, your retirement money, much of your personal household property, a car if it isn't worth much, and public benefits like Social Security and unemployment insurance. Chapter 13 is also known as "wage earner's" bankruptcy. You get to keep your assets, and you pay back some or most of what you owe through a court-ordered plan over a maximum of five years. If you are contemplating bankruptcy, get the professional advice of an attorney and make sure you understand all the ramifications before filing. The new law hiked the cost of going bankrupt to discourage filings.

After Debt

Here's the real question: What lessons do you take away from having carried too much debt and struggling to get rid of it? Will you leave your debt burdens behind and change your money habits? What you don't want to do is go on a roller coaster, zooming once again into too much debt, followed by another stressful period of paying it off, only to take on more debt once your balance reaches zero. The message of frugality and

It's always cheapest to buy a car with cash, but it isn't always practical. Question is, lease or borrow? I'm no fan of leasing. When you lease, you essentially rent a car for three years. You don't own it. You return the car at the end of the lease. Of course, you can buy the car at the end of the lease, but many people simply lease another vehicle. Leasing turns into a world of perpetual car payments. Leasing also encourages buying more car than you need. Leasing is too complicated. It doesn't pass the simplicity test. The Federal Reserve recommends that anyone contemplating a lease should take the following factors into account:

- The agreed-upon value of the vehicle—a lower value can reduce your monthly payment

- Up-front payments, including capitalized cost reduction

- The length of the lease

- The monthly lease payment

- Any end-of-the-lease fee and charges

- The mileage allowed and per-mile charges for excess miles

- The option to purchase at the end of the lease or earlier

- Whether the lease includes "gap" coverage, which protects you in case the vehicle is stolen or totaled in an accident

Got that? Let's keep it simple. Car loans are readily available. Shop for the best terms. You don't want any prepayment penalty, and you don't want to take out a loan longer than three years. Make as big a down payment as you can. Pay the loan off as quickly as possible.

social sustainability supports a lifestyle that isn't fueled by debt. Fact is, you won't feel that you're depriving yourself, which is a big factor behind borrowing too much. Instead, you'll get greater satisfaction focusing on experiences, sharing within your community, and living more the life you want to lead than the life dictated by the relentless rhythm of monthly debt payments.

The Credit Report and Credit Score

Your borrowing history is kept by the three main credit-reporting bureaus. They are Experian, TransUnion, and Equifax. It's important to periodically review your credit reports. You want to make sure the information is accurate. You also want to make sure that no one has stolen your identity. You can't change the past. However, you can dispute in writing any inaccurate or outdated information. If your report contains a mistake, each of the credit bureaus offers a dispute form and steps to follow to fix it. You should also ask the credit bureau to add any missing positive information to your credit history.

By federal law, you can get a copy of your report from each bureau for free once a year, from AnnualCreditReport.com. AnnualCreditReport .com is the only authorized provider for your free annual credit report under federal law. You can get in touch with the outfit online, through a toll-free number (1-877-322-8228), or by mail (Annual Credit Report Request Service, P.O. Box 105281, Atlanta, GA 30348-5281). In other words, ignore TV ads, e-mail offers, and online search results that come up with a different provider offering "free" credit reports. They're trolling to sell services for a fee. Set it up so that you get one report every four months so as to monitor your credit throughout the year. But you can get all three reports at once if you want. You also have the right for a free report if you've been denied a loan.

Your credit score is created out of your credit-reporting history. A credit score is derived from proprietary mathematical formulas, and the

A "credit freeze" or "security freeze" lets you block the disclosure of your credit report by the credit bureaus. It's standard practice for anyone who is a victim of identity theft. But even for those without fraud concerns, a credit freeze can be a sensible strategy. You pay a small fee, typically $10, to freeze your record. You can then thaw it when you are going to borrow some money so a lender can check you out. A thaw typically takes several days and another $10-or-so fee. You'll pay another fee to put it back in the freezer. A freeze does mean you'll have to plan ahead if you're in the market for a new job, apartment, credit card, mortgage, refinancing, and the like. That's fine with me.

number assigned to you tells lenders how risky it is to loan money to you. The higher your credit score, the better the interest rate you'll get, and the more eager lenders will be to do business with you. The lower your score, the higher the interest rate you'll have to pay on a loan, and the harder it is to find a lender.

The eight-hundred-pound gorilla of the credit-scoring industry is a company called Fair Isaac. It's the company behind the FICO score. What goes into your FICO credit score? According to Fair Isaac, 35 percent of your FICO score is based on your payment history; 30 percent on the amounts you owe and on what kind of credit accounts you have; 15 percent on the length of the borrowing history on your accounts; 10 percent on new credit you've taken on; and another 10 percent on the kinds of credit used. The scores range from a top level of 720 to 850, with the lowest level at 500 to 559. In essence, the longer you make your loan payments on time, the better your credit score becomes. Time is on your side if you went through a difficult patch and missed a bunch of payments. Once you've restored good habits, the problems fade into the background and your score climbs higher.

Your credit score matters. You can see the impact of a credit score on borrowing rates from this example drawn from FICO. The traditional thirty-year, fixed-rate mortgage for prime borrowers averaged a bit below

5 percent at the time. The mortgage loan is for $150,000, and the borrower is making a 20 percent down payment on the home.

FICO SCORE	MORTGAGE RATE (%)
720–850	4.760
700–719	4.885
675–699	5.423
620–674	6.573
560–619	N/A
500–559	N/A

The reason for the N/A for the two lowest score levels is that borrowers with such low scores and damaged credit can't qualify for the better loan terms offered on conventional mortgages. They would be pushed into the notorious subprime mortgage market.

I'm not a booster of the credit-scoring business. Too many people worry about learning the tricks of the credit-scoring trade. I'd rather break the tyranny of the credit score. For instance, many borrowers found their credit scores dinged when their bank slashed their credit limits and even closed unused credit card accounts during the Great Recession. The impact of a closed account comes from the effect it has on your ratio of total credit balances to total credit limits. Closing an account lowers your overall credit limit and raises the ratio. The same thing happens if you close an account on your own. It's why a number of financial advisers recommend keeping open unused accounts. I disagree. The tactic doesn't pass the common sense test. Why maintain an account that you don't want, don't need, and don't use? Another reason to close it is that identity theft is a widespread problem. The only real issue is timing. If a major purchase is in your immediate future, such as buying a home, leave your unused accounts alone. It pays to wait to close the accounts until after the deal is done. Then I would get rid of them. The effect on your score is fairly limited anyway, and with good habits your score will bounce back.

That said, the credit-scoring business is an improvement over past prac-

One way to repair a tattered credit record is to take out a "secured" credit card. You open up a special savings account with a bank that issues you a card. Your credit is equal to or somewhat less than the amount on deposit. You will make some interest off your security deposit. Eventually, after showing a pattern of paying off your bills on time, you can usually switch to a traditional—and cheaper—unsecured credit card.

tices. The credit-score computation doesn't include a number of factors, including race, ethnicity, age, salary, and neighborhood. The romanticized banker knew all the people in the community, their strengths and foibles. But in many cases bankers would only lend to people like them, white, married with kids. It was tough to get a loan if you were a member of a minority, an immigrant, a single mother, a single woman with a career, or simply living on the wrong side of the tracks. Fair Isaac also doesn't factor participation in credit counseling into your credit score. That's the right approach.

Plain-Vanilla Financing

Thanks to Elizabeth Warren, the Harvard law professor and chief watchdog of the government's bank-bailout program, the phrase *plain vanilla* has entered the personal-finance lexicon. The idea is to promote straightforward, easily understood loan products, such as a thirty-year mortgage with a fixed interest rate, no prepayment penalty, and no hidden fees. A credit card with clearly defined fees and penalties. A simple, short-term auto loan rather than a lease contract. Plain vanilla is another way of saying, "Keep it simple."

Obviously, I am a big fan of the plain-vanilla movement. I also think the same appreciation of simplicity should carry over to the management of our accounts. Don't clutter up your wallet and your finances with too many accounts. For instance, why have many credit cards? How many cards do you have? One? Three? Five? How many should you have? I can't think of a good reason why anyone wants more than one. An important exception to that rule is having one for personal use and the other for business expenses. It makes record keeping easier. You should also have a debit card. A debit card is an electronic checkbook, and with a debit card you don't take on debt. Consumers are using debit cards more than credit cards these days. In the end, as I've mentioned, the goal is to be debt free. It will take time, especially for those who borrow to buy a home and invest in higher education. But the quicker you are able to live debt free the greater your margin of safety. It's an epic shift that would meet with Mr. Micawber's approval. Remember, as we noted before, Charles Dickens had Micawber say to the young David Copperfield, "Annual income twenty pounds, annual expenditure nineteen nineteen six, result happiness. Annual income twenty pounds, annual expenditure twenty pounds ought and six, result misery."

That's the kind of advice any borrower can appreciate.

CHAPTER 7

Investing the Simple Way

The reward of a thing well done is to have done it.
—Ralph Waldo Emerson

SAVINGS IS WHAT'S LEFT OVER AFTER you've paid the bills, gone grocery shopping, and taken the kids for ice cream. Saving money is hard. If it were easy to save, we wouldn't need a budget or work so hard to develop good financial habits. But investing is easy. Yes, you read that right. No, I haven't lost it (completely).

It's helpful to divide our savings into two broad categories. The first is your safe money. It's usually the money you've set aside for everything from a car breakdown to college tuition bills to blood pressure medication. It also includes the retirement money you don't want at risk to the whims of the market when you say good-bye to your colleagues for the last time. The critical question is whether the money will be there when you need it. You want to place this money in risk-free securities, and all the main safe options rely on U.S.-government backing rather than private-sector promises. The trade-off for no-to-little-risk savings is a minimal return. It's a reasonable trade-off.

The other broad-brush category is investments at risk to the mood of the market casino. Investments such as stocks and bonds fluctuate in value, and while you hope to make a profit on them, you might suffer a loss. Wharton School finance professor Jeremy Siegel has calculated that the stock market has sported an average annual return of 7 percent, since the early 1800s, after adjusting for inflation. But remember, on average Lake Erie never freezes. Sam Savage, consulting professor of management science and engineering at Stanford University, wrote a book *The Flaw of Averages* documenting how plans "based on *average* assumptions are wrong on *average*." Equities rose by 1,300 percent during the long bull market of 1982 to 1999, yet from 1968 to 1982 they went essentailly nowhere to down for over sixteen years. Bonds can be very volatile securities, too.

Investing is critical. Most of us are reluctant plungers in the market these days through retirement savings plans such as the 401(k). We're supposed to figure out how to invest our money for when we retire in ten, twenty, or thirty years. How is the average person to cope with this? That said, in today's world, the biggest mistake you can make is not save and invest for the long haul. The financial penalty for not participating in a long-term savings plan is far bigger than the risk of picking a poorly performing mutual fund. The financial price for procrastinating is that you delay building a margin of safety.

So, fund to the maximum your retirement savings plan at work, such as a 401(k), 403(b), or 457. If you don't have a pension plan at work, set up an IRA or Roth IRA on your own. If you're self-employed, a SEP-IRA or a sole 401(k) is designed with you in mind.

The good news is that a commonsense framework for managing money has emerged over the past half-century. The practical advice is tailor-made for people who work hard, raise a family, and don't think reading at night government-mandated financial filings is enjoyable. The basic ideas were developed by ivory-tower luminaries, such as Nobel laureate Paul Samuelson. The insights were transformed into investment products by practical idealists such as Jack Bogle of Vanguard.

Retirement savings plans may have a single goal—encourage savings for old age—but the system itself is remarkably balkanized. There are all kinds of plans, and many of them have different rules, income limits, and restrictions. Here is a brief rundown of the main retirement plans for employers and individuals.

Employer-sponsored plans

401(k) It's the mainstay retirement savings plan for private companies. In 2009 you could put aside $16,500. That figure will be adjusted for inflation in 2010 and subsequent years (in $500 increments). Pre-tax dollars are set aside from every paycheck and are invested in the plan. The plan offers a number of investment options, mostly mutual funds. Taxes on the savings are deferred until withdrawal. Many companies match a portion of their employee's contribution. If you are fifty or older you can save more than other participants through "catch-up" contributions. Many plans allow employees to borrow from their accumulated savings. The limit on how much can be borrowed is no more than 50 percent of the value of a plan up to a maximum of $50,000. You can't make cash withdrawals until age 59½ without paying a 10 percent penalty, plus any taxes you owe on the tax-deferred savings. 401(k) plans are portable, meaning when you change jobs you can take your tax-deferred savings with you. You can start drawing down your savings after age 59½ and you must begin withdrawals at age 70½. There is also a Roth-401(k). Your contributions are after-tax dollars, but withdrawals are tax free. Most of the other rules are the same.

403(b) These plans, also called tax-sheltered annuities, are geared for teachers, health care workers, public television and public radio employees, and workers at other nonprofit institutions. These plans are similar to 401(k)s, with payroll deduction, mutual fund investment options, employer matches, borrowing provisions, portability, 50-plus catch-up provisions, and withdrawal rules. There is a Roth-403(b).

457 State and local government employees are the main participants in these plans. Legislative changes over the years have brought the 457 largely in line with the 401(k) and the 403(b). Through a quirk in the law anyone with a 401(k) or a 403(b) can double the amount they put into their retirement savings if their employer also offers a 457. There is no Roth version of the 457.

Plans for the self-employed and small business

SEP-IRA A Simplified Employee Pension-Individual Retirement Account is an easy plan for the self-employed and moonlighters. It's also good for small businesses with a small number of employees. As an employer you can contribute 20 percent of your profits (net profit minus one-half of your self-employment tax) up to a maximum of $49,000 in pretax dollars. You can't take out a loan from the money in the account.

Simple-IRA A Saving Incentive Match Plan for Employees IRA is a pension plan for companies with less than one hundred employees. The federal government created SIMPLE's to encourage smaller companies to offer their employees a retirement plan. The contributions are tax deductible and tax deferred. The 2009 contribution limit of $11,500 is adjusted for inflation in 2010 and after. There is a catch-up provision for anyone fifty and older.

Single-employer 401(k) It's a new wrinkle for the self-employed.

You can't have any employees other than a spouse. It can be established as a Roth-type account funded with after-tax dollars or a pretax account. The contribution limits to the 401(k) are the same as regular retirement savings plan. An owner "match" can be added on top of that, but the combined sum set aside can't exceed $49,000 for 2009. The figure will adjust for inflation in 2010 and after. The price tag for being able to sock away more money is greater complexity.

Individual retirement savings plans

Individual Retirement Account. The limit is $5,000 ($6,000 for those 50 and above). You need earned income to contribute to an IRA, but a nonworking spouse can put in the maximum of $5,000 into an IRA. IRA contributions are pretax and the money compounds tax-deferred. You can't take the money out without penalty before age 59½ and you must start making withdrawals at age 70½. Individuals covered by an employer-sponsored pension plan, such as a 401(k), can deduct part or all of their IRA contributions from taxes if their adjusted gross income is under certain limits.

Roth IRA. A Roth is funded with after-tax dollars. There are income restrictions on who can contribute to a Roth. You can withdraw your earnings from a Roth IRA free of taxes as long as the account has been in place for five years and you're over the age of 59½. Unlike a traditional IRA, you never have to make withdrawals from a Roth during your lifetime.

The key rules of investing are:

- You can't consistently beat the market.
- Trading is hazardous to your wealth.
- Managing risk is key.

The practical implications are:

- Keep fees razor thin.

- Own low-cost, broad-based index funds.

- Own quality "full faith and credit" bonds, bills, savings bonds, and the like. Blue chip corporate bonds and tax-exempt securities are good. Steer clear of high-yield, high-risk debt.

With this approach, there's no need to watch for hot stock tips on the business news networks. Don't waste time trolling the Internet for

Don't be deceived by a fierce fight among finance economists

The efficient market theory has held sway among financiers for the past several decades. Among the signature ideas of this theory is the assumption that investors are rational and that stock prices reflect the best estimate of true value. The theory has taken a beating in recent years, and so-called behavioral economists have gained traction. The behaviorists focus on investor psychology and emotions. Investors can go nutty, and they're prone to bouts of enthusiasm and depression. Investors follow the crowd into the latest hot investment, then rush for the exits together. It's a fascinating debate. Yet lost in much of the heated rhetoric and competing research papers is this insight: Both the behaviorists and supporters of the efficient-market theory agree on a set of practical investment principles for individuals. They are the ones outlined in this chapter. From the point of view of individuals and families managing money over a lifetime, it's the areas of agreement that are striking and vital.

investment ideas. You'll also have absolutely nothing of interest to say about investing at a dinner party. But you get to save smart and free up time to do other things that are much more interesting, such as spending time with family and friends, taking risks with your career, and learning more about sustainability.

Investing in the markets has a long history in the United States. Individuals have plunged into the markets at various times in our history. Yet even a brief look at American market history shows how unprecedented is the current embrace of the markets by ordinary workers.

Everybody Ought to Be Rich

The American capital market largely originated with the various debt securities issued to pay for the Revolutionary War. Treasury Secretary Alexander Hamilton put the federal government's credit on sound footing after the war. The new nation's first major stock market boom and bust was in 1791–92. William Duer, a signer of the Articles of Confederation and a friend of Hamilton's, organized a pool of speculators that borrowed heavily to manipulate bank stock prices higher. The speculative frenzy ended when Duer's adversaries joined forces and popped the bubble. Duer was thrown in debtors' prison, where he died several years later. The debacle led to the creation of the first American securities exchange on May 17, 1792. Twenty-four New York brokers and merchants met on Wall Street to sign the "Buttonwood Agreement," a pact that established standard commissions for trading securities.

Wall Street captured popular imagination and loathing in the nineteenth century. It was the era of infamous speculators and robber barons, ruthless operators such as Daniel Drew, Jay Gould, and Cornelius Vanderbilt. Investment bankers such as J. P. Morgan and Jacob Schiff wielded enormous power over industry, especially the railroads, telegraph, and other businesses that knit together a modern national market. Market manipulations were commonplace in what was essentially an exclusive private club.

That is, until the 1920s. The U.S. economy had greatly grown over the previous four decades. The engine of prosperity was the rise of large-scale enterprises that took advantage of mass production technologies and the spread of electricity into factories. The consumer products they produced were bought on credit. Unemployment was low, corporate earnings were healthy, and national confidence was high. Despite several sharp setbacks, the stock market rose by about 700 percent in the twenties.

The stock market captured the imagination of a newly prosperous nation, even though the actual number of individual investors was relatively small. The mass media were full of stories about shopkeepers, cabdrivers, cleaning women, housewives, and other ordinary Americans jumping into the stock market. Frederick Lewis Allen's 1931 book, *Only Yesterday*, an amusing, insightful recounting of the 1920s, memorably tells of New York City subways crowded with riders skimming the financial pages and of loud dinner-table conversations about the latest speculative gambit. John J. Raskob, the General Motors finance chief and a major figure behind the consumer installment-credit revolution, gave a famous interview on stock market investing in a 1929 *Ladies' Home Journal* article with the title "Everybody Ought to Be Rich." He recommended the magazine's readers put just $15 a month (about $189 in current dollars) into good common stocks to build a hefty nest egg over the next twenty years.

In the fall of 1929 the *Saturday Evening Post* published these famous lines:

> *Oh, hush thee, my babe, granny's bought some*
>   *more shares*
> *Daddy's gone out to play with the bulls and bears,*
> *Mother's buying on tips, and she simply can't lose,*
> *And baby shall have some expensive new shoes!*

The mania for stocks ended with the October 1929 stock market crash. During the Great Depression, the Dow Jones Industrial Average plunged 89 percent from its 1929 peak to its 1932 trough. It partially recovered over the next five years, then the Dow tumbled 52 percent between 1937 and 1942.

Wall Street stayed in the doldrums in the 1950s. Memories of the devastating 1930s lingered with the public. So did sordid revelations of shady dealings and illegal activities by Wall Street's leading lights. Professional investors constantly fretted about "another '29" in the early postwar years. The wealthy sought safety in bonds yielding 3 percent, even though stock dividends paid some 6 percent. The new middle class preferred putting its money into banks and thrifts paying depositors about 1.5 percent.

Not until the 1960s did the middle class really embrace stocks again. Glamorous mutual fund money managers such as Gerry Tsai and Fred Carr had hot hands and graced magazine covers. The brokerage house Merrill Lynch became an industry giant by catering to the middle-class saver. But another economic disaster soured people on stocks. Inflation sent the stock market crashing in the early 1970s. The market didn't really recover until the early 1980s, when inflation trended lower and businesses became more competitive, setting the stage for the secular bull market of the eighties and nineties. Once again, the good times attracted hordes of individual investors.

But this time Main Street joined Wall Street thanks largely to an epic change in pensions. Companies retreated from offering their workers expensive traditional "defined benefit" pension plans in favor of low-cost "defined contribution" plans such as 401(k)s. With the defined-benefit pension plan, the employer bears all the investment risk and commits to a fixed payout of money, typically based on a salary-and-years-of-service formula. In contrast, with the 401(k), the 403(b), and similar retirement savings schemes, workers take greater responsibility for their retirement plans and funding arrangements. Employees decide how much money to invest and where to invest it, depending on the limits established by law and the choices offered by the employer. Employees bear all the investment risk. Millions of employees ended up investing in stocks and bonds mostly through mutual funds, and more than half of households now own stocks.

A Tough Deal

Three decades after the rise of the 401(k)-type plan, it's clear that for many people it's a mixed bag. On the good side, it's a vehicle for automatic, tax-deferred savings. The risk is that it demands a lot of employees to pick the right investments. If you can buy high-quality bonds or a no-load stock index fund, great. But be careful about buying individual stocks or actively managed equity funds. Most employees know little about the markets. A steady stream of scholarly research on finance makes a persuasive case that most of us aren't wired to invest well. Behavioral economists have cataloged a long list of systemic mistakes, such as an ingrained tendency to rely on stereotypes; overestimating our ability to predict the future; a willingness to hold on to bad bets because we don't like to feel regret; and a tendency to follow where the herd is going. Benjamin Graham once remarked, "The investor's chief problem—and even his worst enemy—is likely to be himself."

Steven Leuthold, a market historian and longtime money manager, agrees. He looked at the stock market from 1984 through 2000 and found that mutual fund investors did dramatically worse than the overall stock market. The Standard & Poor's 500 Stock Index showed an average annual return of 16.29 percent. The average equity mutual fund investor realized an annual gain of only 5.32 percent. Imagine, during one of the biggest, longest bull market runs in history, mutual fund investors lagged behind even the 5.82 percent return on risk-free U.S. Treasury bills.

What accounts for the miserly return in equity mutual funds? We are nothing like the rational thinking machines described in finance textbooks. Emotions, fads, and biases affect our investment decisions. Many people are far too confident of their stock-picking ability when the market is strong, and much too depressed about their lack of acumen when it spirals lower. Think of the dot-com and the residential-real-estate booms and busts. The basic problem was eloquently captured by Sir Isaac Newton, the great scientist. He lost a small fortune speculating during the South Sea Bubble in the eighteenth century. Newton ruefully remarked after the experience, "I can calculate the motions of the heavenly bodies, but not the madness of people."

The "madness of people" moves at lightning speed. Nowhere has telecommunications and information technology had a greater impact than on the capital markets. European merchant bankers used carrier-pigeon networks in the eighteenth century to get an edge on their rivals. Thanks to the telegraph, the ticker, and the telephone, stock trading in nineteenth-century America went from a local business to a national one dominated by Wall Street. In recent decades, financiers around the world have poured trillions into building proprietary satellite and fiber-optic communications networks that span the globe, and the communications revolution took another giant leap forward with the Internet.

There hasn't been the same degree of progress in our judgment, our ability to make sense of what is happening. "No bell rings when the market changes its emphasis. The market integrates several time scales into a cacophony—or a symphony, depending on the temperament of the listener," wrote master investor Leon Levy in his 2002 market memoir *The Mind of Wall Street.* "Prices respond to the news of the day, to technical factors pertaining to particular stocks; they respond to political events here and abroad; they respond to market players trying to guess how people will react to events; they respond to technological change and shifts in trade policies; they respond to long-term phenomena, such as the aging of baby boomers and trends in capital spending. At one moment, the mood in one aspect of the market may be ebullient, while elsewhere it is morose; the entire market gets swept along by a tide of emotion."

Where Are the Customers' Yachts?

Surely it pays to hire a professional money manager to invest for you, instead? You and I may not know much about investing. But the pros are backed by an army of researchers and analysts comfortable with numbers. They tap into worldwide databases and manipulate powerful algorithms to uncover value in markets. Most individual savers turn to actively managed

A recommended reading list of investment books

Against the Gods: The Remarkable Story of Risk by Peter L. Bernstein. It's a fascinating history of the concept of risk and how managing it became the essence of investing.

A Random Walk down Wall Street by Burton Malkiel. He translates the quantitative, highly abstract insights of modern finance theory into everyday language.

Extraordinary Popular Delusions and the Madness of Crowds by Charles Mackay. Published in 1841, Mackay's book is a powerful indictment of market psychology. In the preface to the 1930s version, the legendary investor Bernard Baruch captured the book's spirit by quoting the German philosopher Friedrich Schiller: "Anyone taken as an individual is tolerably sensible and reasonable— as a member of a crowd, he at once becomes a blockhead."

The Intelligent Investor by Benjamin Graham. It's the best book ever written on investing and the markets. I recommend the version updated with commentary by Jason Zweig, the *Wall Street Journal*'s perceptive columnist.

More Than You Know: Finding Financial Wisdom in Unconventional Places by Michael Mauboussin. He makes abstract finance theory fun with insights drawn from behavioral economics, cognitive science, and complexity research.

Worry Free Investing by Zvi Bodie and Michael J. Clowes. Their basic message is that most people don't want to get rich or, perhaps more accurately, aren't willing to take the kind of gambles that might lead to great riches or end in a visit to bankruptcy court. Most of us want to sustain our standard of living throughout our lives. The way to accomplish that is to limit downside risk—and save a hefty portion of your income every year.

Unconventional Success: A Fundamental Approach to Personal

> *Investment* by David Swensen. It's one of the best books for individual investors looking to manage their money smartly for the long haul.
>
> *The Little Book of Common Sense Investing* by John Bogle. It's a deceptively simple introduction to the basics of a sound investment strategy. I'd recommend it for any beginning investor.

mutual funds to invest their money. Mutual funds take small bits of money from thousands of individuals, pool that money, and invest it in stocks, bonds, cash, or some combination of assets. The bulk of the money is actively traded, meaning the funds are run by professionals who promise to beat the market. The earliest mutual funds appeared in late-eighteenth-century Holland. The first modern mutual fund in the United States was the Boston-based Massachusetts Investment Trust of 1924, better known back then as MIT. Today, approximately seven hundred companies run almost nine thousand mutual funds with over $10 trillion in assets.

That's the promise. Problem is, most actively traded funds don't do well compared to the market, and they charge hefty fees to boot. "Actively managed mutual funds consistently fail to produce superior returns," says David Swensen, the chief investment officer for Yale University's endowment fund and a remarkably successful longtime investor. "When taking sales charges into consideration, the failure of actively managed mutual funds reaches staggering proportions. In the final analysis, the benefits of active management accrue only to the fund management company, and not to the investor."

In 1940, Fred Schwed Jr. asked, with one of the most memorable Wall Street book titles ever, the right question: *Where Are the Customers' Yachts?* It's worth repeating the allegory that starts off the book:

> Once in the dear dead days beyond recall, an out-of-town visitor was being shown the wonders of the New York financial district. When the party arrived at the Battery, one of his guides indicated some handsome ships riding at anchor.

He said, "Look, those are the bankers' and brokers' yachts."

"Where are the customers' yachts?" asked the naive visitor.

Where indeed?

Numerous scholarly studies have documented the relatively poor performance of professional money managers compared to the market averages, such as the Standard & Poor's 500. In essence, a majority of professional money managers do worse than the main benchmark indexes. "When someone says, 'I intend to beat the market,' the market he is talking about is not some neutered beast; it's the sum of all the smartest, toughest minds in this business," says Charles Ellis, the longtime pension and investment consultant. Rex Sinquefield, a longtime finance maven, famously remarked, "There are three classes of people who do not believe that markets work: the Cubans, the North Koreans, and active managers." (It looks as if the Cubans are opening up more to markets, so in the future it may just be the two classes.)

My first experience with how difficult it is to make money in the market came when I was employed by Eliot Janeway. Janeway was a very smart man. As a young journalist at the *Nation, Time,* and *Fortune,* he was part of the New Deal brain trust, along with such powerful figures as Supreme Court justice William O. Douglas, power broker Tommy "the Cork" Corcoran, and the cerebral lawyer Benjamin Cohen. Janeway moved among the famous and powerful. He created multiple careers as a business consultant, columnist, investment adviser, financial newsletter writer, and inveterate wheeler and dealer. I was editor of his two newsletters during the deep recession of the early 1980s.

 You can go to helpforinvestors.org for links on where to check out financial professionals. You can also find out how to report investment fraud, deal with broker bankruptcies, and file mediation claims.

Those were scary years. Inflation was high and rising in the early 1980s. Interest rates were at double-digit levels. Oil and food prices were in the stratosphere. The Soviet Union was at war with Afghanistan. Janeway masterfully peddled doom and gloom all over the country, bellowing at people about the dire straits we were in—and what to do about it. He was widely known as "Calamity" Janeway, but beneath the bluster he had a genuine talent for spotting trends and going against consensus opinion. For instance, he was quick to sense that oil prices had peaked. He was early, too, in grasping that President Reagan would back policies that would lead to much bigger budget deficits than most Wall Street analysts predicted at the time.

Yet for all his brilliance, Janeway's money counsel was ruinous. He charged a lot for his investing advice. He put clients into gold in a big way. His clients and followers did well at first, riding gold all the way up to a high of $850 a troy ounce in early 1980 (the equivalent of more than $2,200 in current dollars). But by 1982 the bull market in gold was over, and it sank into a twenty-year bear market. The bull market in stocks had begun, but Janeway was convinced the stock market rally wasn't sustainable. He kept flogging gold, cajoling clients into sticking with the precious metal and disparaging stocks. Janeway was right many times about many things. But not right enough often enough to beat the market. It's a familiar story.

Aha, responds Wall Street, the trick is to invest with the small number of money managers that do well over time. Some people do consistently beat the market. Look at Warren Buffett, the Oracle of Omaha. Shareholders in his holding company, Berkshire Hathaway, have earned a compound average annual gain of 20.3 percent from 1965 through 2008. That's double the 10.3 percent performance of the main market benchmark, the Standard & Poor's 500 Stock Index—even after a disastrous 2008 for Berkshire Hathaway.

I'm not going out on a limb when I say conventional wisdom is right: Buffett is an investing genius. If you enjoy basketball as I do, he's the money equivalent of Michael Jordan, LeBron James, and Kobe Bryant all rolled into one. He has what Sir Winston Churchill called "the seeing eye,

The mutual fund universe divides into two: load funds and no-load funds. Load funds typically charge a sales levy of 1 to 6 percent of your investment. The load is the commission paid to the broker who advised you to get into a particular fund. Typically, the fee is paid when you buy the fund. Some mutual funds companies offer you the option of paying the fee when you sell (a so-called deferred-sales load). Others may offer a combination of the two.

Let's look at the example of a front-end load. Say I invest $1,000 in an equity mutual fund with a 5 percent load. The mutual fund company gets $50, and $950 goes into my investment. That's why as a general rule loads are a bad deal for investors. There are only two reasons for paying a load. The best motive for purchasing a load fund is to acquire the services of a professional that you really want, and paying the fee is the price of admission. The other reason is that you want professional help choosing a fund. If you do buy a load fund, fork over the money up front.

A no-load fund doesn't impose a sales charge when you invest in a fund or get out of a fund. More of your investment money gets to work right away. You do your own research and invest your own time. To go back to my $1,000 investment, all $1,000 goes into the mutual fund.

All mutual funds charge an operating or management fee. It can vary significantly, from 0.10 to 3 percent. Low fees are better than high fees.

the ability to see beneath the surface of things, to know what is on the other side of the brick wall, to follow the hunt three fields before the throng."

Still, there's a mystery at the core of what Buffett does. His investment methods and philosophy are well-known. He lays them out in clear language and folksy anecdotes in his widely read annual letter to shareholders. His exploits have been covered in depth over the years in books, magazine articles, and newspaper profiles. Yet he still leaves everyone else far behind in the investment sweepstakes. There's a critical element to what he does that even he can't explain. Nobel laureate Paul Samuelson says that John Maynard Keynes—himself an astute investor–once said, "Really, you should buy one stock at any one time. The best one going. And when it's no longer that, replace it by the new best." Well, silly as those sentences sound, it pretty much sums up what Buffett has done in the postwar era. It's a trick few of us can emulate.

The question is, can you pick the next Warren Buffett to manage your money when he is just starting out in the business? Who among the thousands upon thousands of men and women just starting their professional careers managing money in mutual funds, managed accounts, or some other type of investment vehicle will be the next Buffett? The odds are that at least a handful will consistently beat the market over the next half century, and that if you invest with them in their twenties, you'll pocket a handsome sum of money by the time they reach their sixties. But who?

There really isn't any way to find the next superstar. Last year's hot money manager is usually next year's flameout. That won't work as a technique. Even a two- or three-year sizzling performance is no guarantee that next year the manager will do better. The boilerplate is right: Past performance is no guarantee of future performance.

You Can't Beat the Market, So Join It

It's time to develop a simpler approach toward investing that tilts the odds in your favor. It starts with the realization that you can't beat the market. Investing is the most competitive business in the world. Astronomical sums change hands every day around the globe as millions and millions of smart investors (and many more not so smart ones) try to get an edge on the competition. Thanks to hordes of individual investors, equity researchers, mutual fund money managers, journalists, day traders, hedge fund operators, corporate treasurers, pension fund managers, and other institutional investors, stock prices reflect much that is known about companies and the market. Finding neglected diamonds among the cubic zirconia is tough.

The solution is to invest in index funds. Forget about putting money into actively managed mutual funds. You don't need to bother with them. Keep it simple.

Stocks represent ownership shares in a company. You are an owner of General Electric even if you only buy one of its more than 10.6 billion shares outstanding. Similarly, you own a piece of Google if you buy one of its 242 million shares. Changes in corporate earnings, along with the mood of investors, are the main drivers of stock prices. Stocks are volatile, and they can soar into the stratosphere or lose half their value with sickening rapidity.

An index fund duplicates the performance of a particular stock market index. Since 1802, according to Professor Jeremy Siegel, the compound average annual return adjusted for inflation has been 7 percent for stocks, but the yearly returns range widely from bear-market lows to bull-market highs. The most famous equity index fund is the Standard & Poor's 500. It is made up of stocks of the five hundred largest publicly traded U.S. companies. When professional investors say the market is down or up, they're referring to the S&P. A number of other major indexes are the Dow Jones Wilshire 5000, which captures the whole U.S. stock market, the Russell 2000, designed to reflect smaller and medium-size companies, the Europe Asia Far East index (EAFE), and so on. Since we live in a global economy, it's sensible to index both your domestic stock portfolio and your international equity portfolio.

Indexing is commonly referred to as passive investing. No professional money manager is trying to beat the market, rapidly buying and selling stocks. Yet index funds routinely outperform most actively managed funds. Why? A big advantage is their low cost. The annual fee for investing in the Standard & Poor's 500 is some 0.10 percent versus an average of almost 1.5 percent for actively managed funds. Index funds have no research-analyst costs or multimillion-dollar money-manager salaries to pay. Index funds trade stocks infrequently. The stock turnover comes when a stock gets added or dropped from an index through a merger or acquisition, a bankruptcy, or because the keepers of the index make some minor additions and subtractions to reflect broad changes in the economy. The passive approach keeps taxes down, too.

The latter point is often overlooked. To be sure, most of us have our investments in tax-sheltered accounts, such as a 401(k) or IRA. But if you're investing in a taxable account, the case for low fees, little trading, and low taxes is dramatic. Mark Kritzman is president and chief executive of Windham Capital Management, and a teacher at MIT's Sloan School of Management. He's a longtime advocate of indexing. He created an imaginary investor residing in Massachusetts (or any other comparable high-tax state). The investor is in the 35 percent tax bracket. She's presented with three investment options: an index fund with an expected return of 10 percent, an actively managed mutual fund with a 13.5 percent return expectation, and a hedge fund with an expected return of 19 percent. Her time horizon is ten years, then the fund is cashed in. The choice seems obvious, no? Go with the hedge fund and its potential 19 percent return.

Kritzman is a quant jock and he runs through a series of complicated simulations. I'm going to focus on the bottom line. He deducts from returns taxes, transaction costs (the costs associated with buying and selling stocks, for example), and management fees. The index fund return net of all expenses is 8.27 percent, the mutual fund return is 7.82 percent, and the hedge fund 7.61 percent. What accounts for the difference? Well, the main reason is that the expenses incurred by the actively managed mutual fund are more than three times those of the index fund, and the hedge fund expenses are six times higher. You can juggle the numbers in different ways, but clearly cost matters.

To be sure, indexing is "a dull, boring way to be a better investor than many of your friends," says Nobel laureate William Sharpe. "By periodically investing in an index fund," adds Warren Buffett, "the know-nothing investor can actually outperform most investment professionals."

Just ask Robert Wilson. A hedge fund pioneer, Wilson started with $15,000 of his own money in 1949 and parlayed it into a $226 million

The Financial Industry Regulatory Authority (FINRA) is the main independent regulator for securities firms. It offers a mutual fund cost calculator at http://apps.finra.org/fundanalyzer/1/fa.aspx. It's a free Internet tool that lets you compare the total cost of owning a mutual fund and exchange-traded funds. The calculator's estimate of ownership costs includes everything from sales charges to the annual operating expenses paid by investors. Better yet, the calculator also figures out any forgone earnings—money that could have been earned had those fees been invested instead.

fortune when he retired in 1986. His wealth has grown considerably since then. He's now a generous philanthropist, focusing on giving his money away.

When he "retired," Wilson divided his money among roughly twenty aggressive topflight money managers. Remember, he was among the best in the business, he knew the money managers he was choosing, and they all had sterling reputations. Wilson ended up firing fourteen over the years, but kept roughly the same number overall. "Up until the beginning of 1999, I would say that if I'd put half of my money, in fact, I actually did a rough calculation of this, if I'd put half of my money in an index fund—the S&P, the Vanguard fund—and half of my money in two-year Treasury bills, I would have done almost as well as these managers did," he said during an interview with *TheStreet.com* back in 2000. "The problem is . . . in any year, some manager was sort of losing touch and had to be replaced, another manager, who was doing fabulously, had a bad year, and things average out. I found it very frustrating."

What was his advice for the individual investor? "I'd say as a general rule put it in index funds. I don't see why small investors should horse around with money managers."

Socially Responsible Investing and Indexing

Mutual funds that focus on sustainability are increasingly popular. The socially responsible funds share a number of common characteristics. A typical list of concerns includes community, diversity, environment, and human rights. Socially responsible funds avoid investing in a number of products such as alcohol, firearms, gambling, military, and tobacco.

It pays to be tax smart with your investments. That means carefully distributing your stocks, bonds, and other investments between taxable accounts and tax-deferred vehicles such as retirement accounts.

It's easier said than done. The tax code has a lot of wrinkles. For instance, taxes are deferred on contributions to and earnings from 401(k)s and IRAs. Withdrawals are taxed at ordinary income rates. But in a Roth IRA, the contribution is funded with aftertax dollars and the savings are tax-free when withdrawn. Taxes are owed every year in a taxable account, but Uncle Sam plays favorites. Interest earned on bonds by a high-income saver is taxed at the top federal marginal income tax rate. The long-term capital gains tax on an investment held for more than a year is a fraction of that rate.

You can minimize total taxes and maximize returns by putting assets that face the highest taxes into tax-sheltered retirement accounts. Here's an example from James M. Poterba, a Massachusetts Institute of Technology economist: Suppose you put $10,000 into bonds that generate a pretax return of 5 percent per year, and the interest is reinvested at 5 percent. After thirty years in a taxable account, the $10,000 is worth $30,800 if you are in the 25 percent marginal federal tax rate. If the same bonds were in a tax-sheltered IRA and taxed at 25 percent on withdrawal, it would be worth about 9 percent more. But in a Roth IRA, the investment would be worth 45 percent more than in the taxable account. What about stocks? With the low rate on capital gains, the IRA could work against you. Had you put $10,000 in stocks in a taxable account, earned 5 percent a year, sold them in three decades, and paid only capital gains tax, the investment would be worth nearly $40,000. Had that equity investment been made in a traditional IRA, the proceeds would be taxed at the 25 percent rate, leaving you with about $6,000 less. (These examples assume tax rates remain the same during the three decades.) The Roth? Almost $45,000.

The more you save, the more you will boost your returns by paying attention to different tax treatments.

Most funds also invest to reward companies for certain practices or behavior, such as taking sustainability seriously, embracing a diverse workforce, producing safe products, and engaging with local communities.

Ethical investing has a long and rich history, especially within religious communities. For instance, eighteenth-century Quakers refused to invest in the slave trade. As religious groups began investing more in stocks during the nineteenth century, leaders advocated steering clear of companies that profited from sin, such as alcohol and gambling. The Pioneer Fund was created in 1928 to let individuals invest with their beliefs. The ethical investing movement gathered momentum during the Civil Rights movement, resistance to the Vietnam War, and opposition to the apartheid regimes in Rhodesia (Zimbabwe) and South Africa. More recently, socially responsible investing has moved into the investing mainstream with worries over human rights in a global economy, environmental concerns, and a growing desire to work with companies willing to design a business model around sustainability.

The idea of investing with your conscience has long raised hackles on Wall Street and among many financial planners. One reason may be terminology. The phrase *ethical investing* or *socially conscious* investing implies that everyone else is amoral or unethical with his or her money. But the biggest rap on socially responsible investing has been the widespread belief that marrying personal values to an investment portfolio—a noble idea—cuts into returns. In other words, doing good and making money don't mix. Even if that were true, it wouldn't bother many people who care about sustainability. It's a reasonable trade-off.

The thing is, the trade-off doesn't really exist, at least over longer periods. Recent studies find little difference between pooling money to make money and pooling money to make money and express values. For example, Meir Statman, finance economist at Santa Clara University, has in several studies analyzed the performance of the socially responsible equity index funds, socially responsible actively managed equity funds, and actively managed stock funds. His conclusion: The risk-adjusted returns on the socially conscious index funds are roughly comparable to the Standard & Poor's 500 index fund. What's more, the performance of actively managed socially responsible mutual funds is about equal to that of their conventional peers.

In other words, concludes Statman, the best way to fall short when it comes to stock market returns is to pick an actively managed mutual fund, socially conscious or not, over a broad-based index fund. When shopping for a socially responsible index fund look closely at fees. They vary a lot. For instance, some socially responsible index funds charge an upfront load and a steeper-than-expected management fee. In sharp contrast, the Vanguard FTSE Social Index Fund sports an expense ratio of 0.24 percent, with no upfront fee or charge to get out of the fund. Low fees are good.

Your Safe Fixed-Income Money

Let's take a look at your safe money, which goes into fixed-income securities. My main recommendation is always to put this savings into

Exchange traded funds or ETFs are investment vehicles that track indexes. But an ETF is traded like a stock. The most popular ETFs are based on broad stock indexes such as the S&P 500 and the Dow Jones Wilshire 5000. There are also a number of broad-based socially responsible ETFs. It's another way for the small investor to take a plunge into windmill, solar, and other energy alternatives.

Problem is, an explosion of ETFs has sliced and diced the market into smaller and smaller pieces. Intrigued by patents? There's an ETF for you. Think the Austrian economy is poised to rebound? Yes, there's an Austrian ETF. That's why I am wary of ETFs. It's a product increasingly designed for speculation, not investing. I'd be cautious before plunging into an ETF. If you need to make a purchase of a broad-based index all at once, an ETF is fine. It's also a good way to fill out a socially conscious investing portfolio, from alternative energy to sustainability indexes. But for the core of your investing portfolio, the investments that you're adding to over time—just a small portion of each paycheck, for example—then index mutual funds are the more cost-effective choice.

securities backed by a government guarantee and the debts of truly blue chip companies.

The bond world is incredibly complex. Wall Street rocket scientists have devised all kinds of exotic securities. Many of them went bust during the Great Recession. High-yield, high-risk securities with all kinds of bells and whistles don't belong in most portfolios. The question "Whom can you trust?" in bond land isn't an idle query. Again, let's keep our fixed-income investing simple. The combination of a margin-of-safety framework and keeping it simple argues for investing mostly in "full faith and credit" fixed-income securities. With U.S. Treasury securities and FDIC-insured accounts there is no risk of default. I would also stick with the debt of blue chip companies. State and local governments issue tax-exempt securities, better known as municipal bonds. I like conservative "general obligation" bonds that are backed by the state and local governments' taxing authority. A big advantage of investing in fixed-income securities is that safe bonds will protect your savings and earn you a rate of interest. Bonds make it easier for you to plan your financial life.

With a fixed-income security, you are lending money to the issuer. The amount you've lent is the principal or face value of the loan. The IOU is outstanding until a certain time, called the maturity date. You get paid interest for the money, and the rate is called a coupon or yield. For instance, if I buy a ten-year U.S. government bond for $1,000 with a coupon of 5 percent, I get a yearly interest payment of $50 and my $1,000 back at the end of ten years.

Of course, interest rates change all the time. Investors may believe the rate of inflation is going to go higher or lower, they may flee for the safety of debt or abandon it for higher returns elsewhere. Throughout all the turmoil in the bond market, think of the interest rate and the bond price as two ends of a seesaw. When interest rates rise, bond prices fall, and when interest rates go down, bond prices rise. Take our ten-year bond at 5 percent. Interest rates rise to 6 percent, and I have to sell it. I will get less than $1,000 for my bond. But now, let's imagine that interest rates fall to 4 percent and I still have to sell. My bond is worth more than $1,000. However, changes in interest rates are less of a concern if you hold on to a fixed-income security until it matures. According to Professor Siegel, the inflation-adjusted return on long-term government bonds has been 3.5 percent. The return on short-term government securities or bills over the past two centuries is 2.9 percent. Bonds are less volatile than stocks, but more volatile than bills.

One strategy when owning individual bonds is to create a "ladder." The idea is to invest in U.S. Treasuries or certificates of deposit with different maturities. For example, you plunk down $10,000 each to buy one-year Treasuries at 2 percent, two-year at 3 percent, three-year at 3.5 percent, and five-year at 4 percent. Six months from now interest rates go up. You have some short-term debts that will soon mature, and you can reinvest that at a higher rate. If rates fall, you're still earning a better return on your higher-yielding fixed-income securities.

The Main Safe Places for Money

Savings accounts at federally insured institutions are a classic parking place for money. The Federal Deposit Insurance Corporation insures bank accounts, and the National Credit Union Shares Insurance Fund insures credit unions. Government insurance is limited to $250,000, although it's relatively easy to put a multiple of that sum at the same bank and get it insured. To be sure, the $250,000 limit is scheduled to return to its previous $100,000-per-depositor limit on January 1, 2014. I expect Congress will make the temporary increase permanent at some point. Online banks often offer better rates to savers since they aren't paying for brick-and-mortar costs. Savings at community development banks are recycled into the local area.

Certificates of deposit are insured fixed-income investments sold by banks, savings and loans, and credit unions. CDs typically range from three months to five years. You get a higher interest rate by locking up your money for a longer period. If you take the money out early, you'll still get your principal, but you'll pay a penalty on interest earnings. These are low-risk, low-return investments. Again, at a federally insured financial institution CDs are backed up to $250,000.

Investors from around the world have sought safety and security in

U.S. Treasury fixed-income securities. You can buy Treasury bills, notes, and bonds online directly from the U.S. Treasury at treasurydirect.gov with a minimum investment of $100. The Treasury offers a wide range of maturities ranging from one month to a year for bills, two years to ten years for notes, and thirty years for bonds. Treasuries are ideal for a buy-and-hold-until-maturity strategy.

The most important U.S. government bonds for investors are Treasury Inflation-Protected Securities, better known as TIPS. These securities are the long-term saver's friend. One of the biggest risks faced by savers is that inflation will erode the value of money over time. Even small rates of inflation, say, in the 1 to 3 percent range, reduce the purchasing power of savings. Many economists reasonably fear that inflation could go much higher than that following the extraordinary actions the Federal Reserve took to bail out the banking system and to avoid a depression. Savers can create a simple risk-free margin of safety by investing in TIPS. Inflation-indexed bonds come in five-, ten-, and twenty-year maturities. TIPS offer a fixed interest rate above inflation, as measured by the consumer price index. An additional advantage of TIPS is that they protect against deflation—a decline in the overall price level of goods and services—by offering a "deflation floor" that protects principal value during deflation.

TIPS have two main drawbacks. The first is that Uncle Sam requires owners of TIPS in a taxable account to pay income taxes on their inflation-adjusted gains before getting any of the inflation-adjusted money at maturity. The easy way to invest in TIPS and avoid the tax problem is to own them in a tax-deferred retirement savings account, such as a 401(k) or IRA. The other problem is that for a variety of legal and regulatory reasons, you can't buy TIPS directly from the U.S. Treasury for your retirement savings account. You have to pay a broker to do it for you. It's worth it, however.

Taxes aren't an issue with I Savings Bonds, the federal government's other inflation-protected security. These bonds allow your money to compound tax-deferred until they are cashed in. There are no commission costs when buying or selling them. I-bonds redeemed before the five-year mark forfeit the three most recent months' interest, but after five years there is no penalty at redemption. The only drawback to I-bonds is that you can't buy very much at a time. Savers can purchase $10,000 worth a year—$5,000 online from the Treasury and $5,000 in paper bonds bought at a bank.

Don't Put All Your Eggs in One Basket

We're almost done with the ingredients behind a simple investing framework. The fundamental notion informing modern finance is the proposition that returns are only earned as compensation for taking on risk. Stocks are riskier than bonds since equities represent the uncertain rewards for entrepreneurship. Bonds are slightly less risky. They are long-term contracts that spell out when borrowers must make principal and interest payments. Despite the hours people spend agonizing over mutual funds and worrying over the market's every twist, "asset allocation" is the main determinant of your portfolio's performance. Asset allocation is a fancy way of saying how you divide your money among the investment options available to you. The essence of asset allocation is the inevitable trade-off between risk and return. The more risk you are

---

Some savers find it easier to own multiple CDs backed by the FDIC by buying so-called brokered CDs. A broker will take, say, a $500,000 investment and buy five $100,000 CDs. All the monitoring and paperwork of the account are in one place. But brokered CDs have some rather peculiar twists. For one thing, you have to hold them until maturity. If you do need the money, your broker can only sell the CD on the open market, and depending on the financial environment, you could lose some of the principal value. For most of us, the CDs we can buy from a bank or local credit union are best.

willing to take, the greater your chance for higher returns—or loss. And vice versa.

One of the wrong investing mantras of the recent decades was that stocks aren't actually all that risky. Sure, we were told, stocks are more volatile than bonds. But over time stocks became less and less risky to own. They turned into the equivalent of diamonds while bonds were cubic zirconium. The height of this thinking came with the 1999 book *Dow 36,000* by James K. Glassman and Kevin A. Hassett. "The Dow Jones industrial average was at 9,000 when we began writing this book," they noted in their introduction. By their calculations "in order for stocks to be correctly priced, the Dow should rise by a factor of four—to 36,000 . . . The Dow should rise to 36,000 immediately, but to be realistic, we believe the rise will take some time, perhaps three to five years."

Oops. A closer look at the data suggests that the notion of stocks as a riskless security over the long haul is wrong. Bonds have often outperformed stocks for ten-year periods. Before 1871, stocks did not always do better than bonds even with a thirty-year time horizon, notes Robert Shiller, economist at Yale University. You don't even have to

I'm not a fan of buying individual stocks for long-term savers. That's for fun. The money you're investing is your "play" money or "mad" money. Whatever you call it, it comes from the same budget line as going to a restaurant and heading off on vacation. It's money you can afford to lose. You aren't putting your retirement, your children's college education, or savings at risk to your stock-picking prowess. If that's the case, take an occasional flier and match wits with the market. I'd recommend buying individual stocks in a taxable account. Uncle Sam will share your pain by allowing you to take a tax write-off if you're wrong. But if you're right and you own the security for more than a year, you'll pay a low capital gains rate on the profit.

reach into the history books. From 1983 to 2008, the annual total return on stocks was 9.8 percent a year versus an 11 percent average annual return on Treasury bonds. "There is no predestined rate of return, only an expected one that may not be realized," says Laurence Siegel, director of investment policy research at the Ford Foundation. "The risk of holding stocks, then, is the possibility that in the long run, returns will be terrible."

To finance professionals, risk is synonymous with volatility. It's not a bad perspective. High volatility increases the odds that you'll suffer a loss if you need to sell an asset to raise money. But that isn't what risk means to the average person saving in a retirement plan, a family investing in a 529 college-savings account, a household struggling to salt away some money in an emergency savings fund. Risk is not having the money you need to pay your mortgage, to send your children to college, to live as well in your nineties as you did in your fifties. If you have a lot of money, then you can withstand a great deal of volatility before your basic standard of living is really lower. To take an extreme example, the families of billionaires Warren Buffett and Bill Gates weren't affected by the bear market and the recession. But that's not true for most of us. "Risk in many ways is the probability of not reaching the things that you want to reach, not meeting your goals," says financial planner Ross Levin.

That's why focusing on asset allocation concentrates the mind on a related idea, diversification, the sensible notion of not putting all your eggs in one basket. It's among the most celebrated concepts in modern finance. Economist Harry Markowitz even got a Nobel Prize for turning your parent's oft-repeated advice into mathematical equations. Diversification both reduces investment risk and increases the odds that you'll earn a decent return over time. The trick is to put your money into assets that don't necessarily march in lockstep. You want some assets that zig while others zag. To be sure, diversification doesn't provide much shelter in the worst moments of a major financial crisis, such as during the credit crunch and bear market of 2008–09 and the financial trauma of 1973–74. But outside of the immediate experience of the extremes, diversification has been shown to work again and again.

You shouldn't just think about the risks attached to different kinds of investments. Other aspects of your life play an important role. For instance, a tenured university professor with job security can take on more financial risk than a salesman on commission. A conversation between Zvi Bodie and Jack Bogle illustrates the point. They were discussing risk and diversification. Bodie mentioned that his son-in-law works on Wall Street in a high-risk job with lots of earnings volatility. The odds of making oodles of money are high, but so is the risk of getting laid off or suffering a sharp loss of income.

> BODIE: I say to him over and over again, "You want to be all in fixed income." . . .
>
> BOGLE: . . . You're totally right. Did you persuade him?
>
> BODIE: Yes.
>
> BOGLE: I'm amazed, because if you're in that business, you think trees grow to the sky.
>
> BODIE: I was very forceful because he is in charge of my three-year-old granddaughter, who is the most precious thing in my life right now.

Bodie's son-in-law created a margin of safety for his family by investing in fixed-income securities. It offset the risk inherent in his job.

Money market funds are no longer a safe enough parking place for cash. The industry doesn't want to acknowledge it. Regulators are trying to avoid the issue. Yet for many conservative savers it's simply too risky a product.

It's hard to imagine now, but the money fund was one of the great innovations from the Age of Inflation. In the late seventies

and early eighties, it was the hottest investment for middle-class savers. Regulations at the time prevented banks from offering savers anything over 5.25 percent. But market interest rates were at double-digit levels. Money funds could pay those rates—10 percent, 11 percent, and so on.

Longtime financial journalist Joseph Nocera says the question at the time wasn't "Do you dare to risk your money in such a fund?" It was "How could you not risk your money in a money fund?" In 1980, investors had poured $84 billion into money funds. Two years later, that sum had swelled to $200 billion, says Nocera.

Money funds gradually evolved into a staid investment haven for cash. The business manages more than $1 trillion for individual savers. You always earn a market rate of interest and you can write checks off your account. The industry pledged that a dollar invested in a money fund would be worth a dollar no matter what. It worked for a long time.

That is, until the fall of 2008. The industry broke its word during the darkest days of the credit crunch. When money market fund values started falling below a buck, taxpayers had to rescue the industry. You can't trust the money fund "We won't break a buck" pledge anymore. How do we know our savings won't vaporize during the next financial crisis? We don't. The money in a fund is at risk.

There are good reform ideas out there. Jane Bryant Quinn, the dean of personal-finance journalists, has called for a dramatic overhaul of the business. Money funds that want to say a dollar is a dollar should become like banks with government insurance. Funds that don't want to go that route should say share values will fluctuate. There's nothing wrong with that. Just make it clear that there's a speculative element to the investment.

For now, I trust government insurance. I know my emergency savings are guaranteed even if my bank goes belly up. The same can't be said for money funds. Caveat emptor.

A "Rules-of-Thumb" Portfolio

The late financier Fischer Black noted that with conversation and experience people evolve relatively sophisticated rules of thumb. "They share their rules of thumb with each other," he wrote. "Over time, I expect that transmission through the media and through the schools of scientific ways of interpreting evidence will gradually make the rules of thumb more sophisticated." The first investing rule of thumb is that the fixed-income portion of your portfolio should equal your age. If you are thirty years old, fixed-income securities should be 30 percent of your portfolio; fifty-five years old, the fixed-income portion can be 55 percent of your portfolio. Of course, this is just a starting point. You can decide to be more or less conservative, depending on your circumstances. TIPS, Treasury bills, and notes are a terrific fixed-income foundation for long-term savings plans. Certificates of deposit and savings accounts are easy to establish in taxable accounts.

The equity portion of the portfolio is composed of domestic and international index funds. It's common financial advice that most Americans should invest 10 to 30 percent of their equity portfolio overseas. The idea of investing overseas to cushion swings in the U.S. market has fallen into disfavor. The world used to be made up of national markets, and the relationship or correlation between countries was relatively weak. Investors could both reduce the risk of their portfolios and enhance returns through geographic asset allocation. But with goods, services, capital, and labor crossing the globe as never before, the correlation between the U.S. stock market and foreign bourses has tightened considerably. There's no question that seemingly local events can reverberate throughout the world economy with greater force than before. That's what happened during the global credit crunch. Stock markets everywhere fell sharply.

Still, economies and markets are far from marching in lockstep for any length of time. And for anyone with strong nerves and time on their side the prospects of putting some money at risk directly into the global economy is enticing. Imagine, in 1820, India and China produced 50 percent of the world's gross domestic product. They now account for about a fifth, but that percentage will grow with time. Similarly, Vietnam, Malaysia, and Indonesia are embracing growth. So are Brazil and Chile. For long-term investors the strategy that seems to make the most sense in a global economy is a global one.

That's it. You're essentially deciding how to divide two pots of money. One pot is broad-based equity index funds, domestic and international. The other is your fixed-income securities. You can build a whole household portfolio around a sustainability and socially responsible investing theme with this approach, too. The equity portion goes into broad-based sustainable indexes, and the fixed-income portion is largely invested in the insured accounts of community development banks and credit unions. Either way, it's a conservative savings strategy for all economic seasons and financial markets.

While you're playing around with the percentages, you should look at your household portfolio as a whole. We all segregate our assets by their purpose—retirement, college, emergency savings, and so forth. This kind of "mental accounting" is useful. It makes it easier to save. But it can also deceive. Here's why: Let's say you've saved $100,000 in your college education account. Your child is going off to college in five years, and you have divvied up the portfolio into 20 percent equity and 80 percent fixed income. You also have $100,000 in a retirement account, split into 75 percent equities and 25 percent bonds. The asset allocation in each account sounds about right to you on its own. But taken all together, your overall asset mix is 52 percent fixed income and 48 percent equity. That may be too risky a portfolio for you, or too conservative.

The Investing Trinity

You may have heard that the old rules of saving and investing no longer hold. The strategies of buy-and-hold, dollar-cost averaging, and rebalancing a portfolio have fallen into disfavor. The reason is the carnage visited by the

2010 is fast becoming the equivalent of a Roth IRA conversion gold rush. Here's why: Up until 2010, you could only convert a traditional IRA into a Roth IRA if your modified gross adjusted income was under $100,000. The income limit lifts in 2010. When you convert from an IRA to a Roth you owe income taxes on the amount converted. The reason is a traditional IRA is funded with pretax dollars while a Roth is funded with after-tax dollars but withdrawals are tax free in retirement. Well, the 2010 conversion amount may be included as taxable income in 2011 and 2012. That helps spread out the tax bite. It's a one-time perk.

To convert or not to convert, that is the question. There are many factors to consider, but for many people the answer will be yes. The benefit of tax-free withdrawal is huge. The argument for converting strengthens the longer your money can compound after conversion and before retirement. It's also important to have other savings on hand to pay the tax bill. It doesn't pay to convert if you need tax-deferred savings to pay the tax. Another advantage of the Roth is there is no required minimum distribution at age 70½ as there is with a regular IRA. For those with substantial assets converting to a Roth may make financial sense simply from an estate planning perspective.

Still, there are many twists and turns to this conversion story. For instance, should you pay the tax tab in 2010 or spread it out over two years depends on whether you believe the money you make off the delayed payment will offset the risk of a higher tax bill. One place to get started researching the economics of conversion for your household is at the Web-based calculator offered at rothretirement.com. Another is at finance.cch.com/sohoApplets/RothTransfer.html.

bear market on savings. It seems the investment trinity did nothing to stop the financial damage. While few safe havens existed during the downturn, the wrong lesson is to move away from three time-honored margin-of-safety investment strategies.

Buy and Hold

Remember, you don't have a clue what any investment will do going forward, and neither do the experts. That's why I believe essentially in a buy-and-hold approach that avoids market timing. Instead, your portfolio becomes more financially conservative over time as you age. For instance, investors earned a real 2 percent average annual return on their equity investments during the 1930s, according to Ibbotson Associates, a Morningstar company. But they pocketed a real 7.1 percent on their government bonds and 2.7 percent on short-term Treasury bills. Yet during the 1950s, investors earned a real average annual return of 16.8 percent on stocks, while losing 2.2 percent on bonds and 0.3 percent on bills. What will returns be over the next decade? No one knows, but trying to time the market is a waste of effort. "Timing is a tough business," says Nobel laureate Paul Samuelson. "It's easy to sell, but then you have to know when to get back in—and we know that hardly anyone is good at it."

Use Dollar-Cost Averaging

Technically, dollar-cost averaging means putting the same amount of money into an investment regularly over a long period. Let's say you are putting $100 a month into a retirement savings plan or a college fund. When the market is up, you can buy only ten shares. When the market is down, you can buy twenty shares. The real benefit of dollar-cost averaging is that it takes emotion—fear, greed, and panic—out of investing. You are dollar-cost averaging in retirement savings plans such as 401(k)s and 403(b)s, since a portion of your paycheck is regularly invested in the markets.

Rebalance Your Portfolio Regularly

The other market truism is that regularly rebalancing your portfolio gives you a higher return with lower risk. Let's say you're fifty years old and you have half your money in a total stock market equity index fund, and half in TIPS. Prices change throughout the year, and over time your portfolio becomes 60 percent stocks and 40 percent bonds. Should you accept the market's judgment or rebalance your portfolio to get back to your original risk profile? The typical advice is to rebalance whenever the portfolio gets 7 to 10 percent away from your asset allocation. But, I think that's too much work for an uncertain return. We're trying to keep this as simple as possible without doing damage. Jason Zweig, the savvy financial columnist at the *Wall Street Journal*, after running through several different rebalancing scenarios, concluded that once a year is plenty. "Pick a date that will never vary and that you will always remember, like your birthday," he says. He's right about once a year, but I rebel against spending my birthday going over money. Financial planner Paula Kennedy agrees that once a year is enough, but she picks New Year's Day since she isn't a college football fan—a much better idea.

A wonderful passage *in Reminiscences of a Stock Operator* written in 1923 by Edwin Lefevre captures the essence of rebalancing. Lefevre tells this story: Somebody asked Baron Rothschild, the great merchant banker, wasn't it difficult to make money on the bourse (the French stock market)? The baron replied that "on the contrary, he thought it was very easy." "That is because you are so rich," objected the interviewer. "Not at all," said the baron. "I have found an easy way and I stick to it. I simply cannot help making money. I will tell you my secret if you wish. It is this: I never buy at the bottom and I always sell too soon."

Since we don't know what the markets will do I suggest calibrating

> ### Total return.
>
> To answer the question "How are your investments doing?" the best measure is "total return." For stocks, the total return comes from the sum of dividend payments plus any price appreciation—or loss. With bonds, the total return is based on interest payments plus price changes. In addition, you want any return figures adjusted for inflation, especially for long-term investments.

your long-term investment strategy to the rhythm of your life. You know when your children are off to college and around what time you might think about putting in fewer hours on the job. These life transitions will involve a shift in your investment strategy. It makes a lot more sense to pay attention to what is changing in your household than to try and follow the lead of the pied pipers of Wall Street. And live your values. The notion of investing with values is powerful.

Oh, one last thing. Never, ever used borrowed money to invest in the market. Period.

CHAPTER 8

Live Long and Prosper

*This time, like all times, is a very good one if we but know
what to do with it.*

—Ralph Waldo Emerson

AMERICANS ARE GETTING OLDER. THE WOODSTOCK generation, the 76 million or so baby boomers born between 1946 and 1964, is going gray. In 2007, Maryland teacher Kathleen Casey-Kirschling—the nation's first boomer, born in Philadelphia on January 1, 1946—filed for her Social Security benefits. The elderly are living longer than before. Average life expectancy is about seventy-eight years, up from sixty-one years in 1935 when Social Security began.

Yet rather than celebrate, many Americans, it seems, are gripped with foreboding over the prospect of living longer. Americans aren't saving enough for retirement. Social Security is under financial stress. Corporate America is cutting back on traditional pensions, while state and local government pension funds are underfunded relative to the benefit promises made to current and future retirees. The swelling ranks of the elderly will send medical costs spiraling out of control. The gloom only deepened during the Great Recession, especially among boomers who watched their 401(k)s and their homes wither in value. Job losses slashed the household incomes of many working families. The sense grew that aging retirees, instead of being able to savor the good life during their golden years, faced the prospect of eking out an existence reminiscent of William Butler Yeats's bleak picture of old age as a "battered kettle at the heel" and "dull decrepitude."

The conventional distress is overdone. The story of an aging society is far more optimistic. Yes, the public-policy challenges of strengthening America's badly frayed retirement and health care systems are real. The solutions will unfold in coming years. But living longer should be celebrated. It's an opportunity, not a catastrophe. The pessimists are missing a profound shift in our vision of the good life in old age. They discount too readily the embrace of savings, frugality, and sustainability. They underestimate our creativity and resilience. They don't appreciate how sustainability may change much of modern life for the better.

The "Retiring" of Retirement

Economic downturns often accelerate social and economic change. In the latter part of the nineteenth century and in the early twentieth century, the country moved from a rural, farm economy to an urban, industrial one. The wealthy associated old age with leisure, but for everyone else it often meant involuntary unemployment and a humiliating dependence upon family, charity, or community organizations for shelter and food. Worst of all, old age could lead to the poorhouse, a charitably intentioned but much feared institution. Policy reformers agitated for decades for a government-backed financial safety net for the nation's elderly.

Not much happened until the Great Depression. It was an economic disaster for families, especially the elderly, "as they watched their hard-won assets vanish, and with them their hopes for an independent and secure old age," write historians Carole Haber and Brian Gratton in *Old Age and the Search for Security*. Traditional middle-class objections to a national safety net crumbled during the Depression. President Roosevelt signed Social Security into law in 1935. "The real or incipient collapse of individual households helps to explain the widespread popularity of Social Security," say Haber and Gratton.

Our image of the good retirement is still shaped by the early decades after World War II. The poverty rate among the elderly plunged thanks to Social Security. Older Americans gained universal health care coverage with Medicare in 1965. Large corporations offered their workers defined-benefit pension plans based on a salary-and-years-of-service formula. In these years retirees developed a distinct lifestyle featuring mass migration to Sunbelt communities, travel in RVs and bus tours, long mornings on the golf course, and enjoying other recreational pursuits. The transformation was a stunning achievement. "For most individuals retirement is no longer a time of withdrawal from all activities and of dependence on family and friends; rather, it is a time of discovery, personal fulfillment, and relative independence," writes MIT economist Dora L. Costa in *The Evolution of Retirement*. "In the past, such an experience of retirement was limited to the wealthy few that could afford it. Now, it is an option available to the majority of workers."

Today, the economics of retirement are changing again. The core difference revolves around work. The essence of the old retirement was quitting work, saying good-bye to your workmates for the last time. That's why saving for retirement became almost a national obsession in recent decades. How could you afford to live a life of leisure for nearly three decades if you didn't save huge sums of money in your 401(k) plan? The message of the Great Recession: Most of can't save enough for old age. We will end up working well into our golden years. The history of retirement is giving way to a story about work in old age.

Earning a paycheck in your later years is significant to the bottom line. Pocketing even a slim income allows retirement portfolios to compound over a longer time. Take this calculation by economist Robert Shackleton of the Congressional Budget Office, which posits a married couple is in their early sixties earning $100,000 pretax a year in 2004. They'll need nearly $66,000 a year after taxes to replace 80 percent of their preretirement income. (The 80 percent is a standard rule of thumb in this kind of retirement calculation.) If both retire at age sixty-two, they'll receive more than $25,000 a year in total Social Security benefits and require a portfolio of at least $891,000 to generate the income they need to live the good life through their normal life expectancy. But if our couple wait until age sixty-six to retire, their Social Security benefits go up and the time for which they need to bank money shrinks, so $552,000 in savings will suffice. Retire at age seventy? All they require is a portfolio worth some $263,000. And so on. Says Ross Levin, the certified financial planner, "By working, you don't need to save as much, and you don't have to live off your portfolio for so long."

Yet the labor-longer-into-old-age "retirement" strategy involves more than putting in extra years on the job. It will change the way we think about savings. A savings margin of safety is the resource for taking risks with career and job. It gives people the flexibility to find out what they really love to do and the means to reshape the balance between work, family, and community. Savings is the practical safety net that supports the mindfulness of social sustainability and the values it promotes. Savings will be less about retirement and more about funding changes throughout life. "The new goal is to have sufficient assets to liberate yourself to work," says Marc Freedman, head of Civic Ventures, a nonprofit that encourages people to launch second and third careers. "You save not to have freedom from work, but freedom to do the work you want."

To be clear, this doesn't mean you shouldn't take full advantage of any retirement savings plan offered at work or one that you set up on your own. You should. But much of our thinking and advice about savings has been too narrowly focused on the last third of life and too dominated by the Wall Street investment perspective. The New Frugality liberates savings to help us explore life's larger questions throughout our years.

Making the Transition

The shift in managing our retirement builds on the realization that we're better educated and living longer. Disabilities among the elderly are declining, thanks to a combination of healthier lifestyles and medical advances. Surveys have repeatedly shown that a majority of Americans say they expect to be gainfully employed full- or part-time or even start their own businesses, late in life. They're going to get their wish.

More than making ends meet, work is physically and mentally energizing for many people. The office and factory are social environments, with birthday celebrations and coffee klatches, friends and acquaintances, people to swap gossip and stories with, neighbors to commiserate with over divorce and to congratulate on pregnancy. Of course, it's likely that you'll want to move on to a different employer, paid activity, or volunteer opportunity when you're older. But that doesn't mean you won't want to work. "For most people work is a community," says Professor Statman of Santa Clara University.

Work is a place of ongoing education. The importance of the job as classroom came home to me in the early 1990s. I participated in a seminar organized by the late Columbia University economist Jacob Mincer. A labor economist, Mincer was one of the University of Chicago–trained economists, along with such luminaries as Theodore Schultz and Gary Becker, who developed the modern theory of human capital. The seminar focused on the role that education played in widening income inequality during the eighties. Among the participants was Fischer Black, the legendary scholar who co-created in 1973 the main method financiers still use to value options—the Black-Scholes model. At the time he

---

Check out Civic Ventures at civicventures.org. The social entrepreneur Marc Freedman founded the nonprofit to encourage baby boomers to find work they love and to make a difference. His insight is that experienced workers can use their talents to address serious social problems, from sustainability to homelessness. The Web site offers everything from stories by people who have made the transition to original research. It's inspiring and not just for aging boomers.

was a partner at Goldman Sachs, a key member of the investment bank's quantitative brain trust. The conversation kept revolving around the gap between earnings of high-school-educated workers and college-educated workers. Black said nothing for a long time. Suddenly, if I remember right, he said, "Why are we talking about school so much? What you learn on the job is nine to eleven times what you learn at school. That seems a reasonable estimate to me."

The conversation paused. We all nodded in agreement. Then we went back to talking about education and inequality. Reflecting back, we should have spent more time on his insight. The benefits of work aren't just social. It's learning on the job that keeps the mind active. Many places of employment should be called "Workplace U."

The benefits are huge even if you don't earn an income. For instance Carol Thompson had been a licensed clinical social worker with a private practice and a specialty dealing with child-custody cases for the court in the Bay Area. Her work was rewarding, but draining. So, after forty years on the job she looked forward to leaving it all behind her. But then what? One day, while taking a favorite stroll through the University of California's Botanical Garden in Berkeley, she noticed a call for volunteers. She signed up and soon started taking courses in horticulture at Oakland's Merritt Community College. "There is something really stimulating, but humbling, about starting something new," said Thompson back in 2003 when we talked. "It's really an anti-Alzheimer thing to do."

Of course, our perspective on retirement is changing for less happy reasons. A good number of older folks were forced back into the job market after their retirement savings had been ravaged by recession and bear markets twice in eight years. Others put off retiring, worried that they wouldn't have enough to live comfortably. Household budgets among the elderly are squeezed by rising out-of-pocket health care bills, too. Not all senior citizens will be physically and financially healthy in their older years. The comedian George Burns used to get a laugh saying, "Don't stay in bed, unless you can make money in bed." For too many people it isn't a joke.

Call it the Social Security "two step." If you retire early and take a reduced monthly benefit, you can change your mind, reapply, and get the bigger payments that go to those who wait to collect benefits. Of course, there is a catch. You must send the government a check covering the benefits you've been paid (without interest or adjusting for inflation).

Professor Kotlikoff ran numbers for a couple who retire at sixty-two. They have $300,000 in savings, and an additional $100,000 each in retirement assets. They want their money to last until they're one hundred. If they apply for benefits at sixty-two, each gets $17,921 a year.

Fast-forward eight years. Had they waited until age seventy to file, they would get $31,005 each, for a total of $62,010 a year. To get those higher payouts at this point, the formula requires them to pay $118,957 each. That's a big check, and it's why the technique only works for some people. Still, it's worth knowing about. To get that same payout by buying the cheapest commercial annuity would cost them 40 percent more than writing a check to the Social Security Administration, calculates Kotlikoff.

A more practical approach for some aging workers may be "claim and suspend." If you voluntarily suspend your Social Security payments, you'll earn retirement credits that will permanently increase your future monthly benefits. It can be a smart strategy if you earn enough to support yourself without the Social Security money. The higher benefits are valuable since they're payable for life and protected against increases in the consumer price index. You can elect to suspend if you are at your full retirement age but not yet seventy.

Investing in Education and Networks

The new retirement means our definition of savings and investing should move beyond traditional assets such as stocks, bonds, and a home. It should include education, on-the-job training, and networking. Have some fun and dream about what you'd like to do in the next stage of life. Once you're drawn to an idea, invest in the skills you'll need to turn that dream into reality. The return on investment won't happen overnight. But it will move you toward where you want to be. "What is it that you want to do?" asks Ralph "Jake" Warner, the founder of Nolo.com, the self-help legal organization. "Go back to school and attend some classes. It can change your life."

That's what Fred Henry did. By the early 1990s, he had worked for three decades at Bechtel Corp., the giant engineering and construction company, and was a project manager in the company's power-plant business. Sales were down, and Fred, in his late fifties, with a Harvard MBA, was itching for a change. He mulled over different options for building on his Bechtel experience. However, on an airplane flight he read an article about a financial planner and said to himself, "That's what I want to do." He enrolled in financial-planning courses at UCLA, left Bechtel, and became a certified financial planner based in Torrance, California, with a book of clients. "I wanted to get out of corporate life and do something I'm interested in and be independent," he told me several years ago.

Schooling is important. But so is networking. Many people nearing retirement are eager to do work that benefits their community. It's time for a change. Problem is, good intentions and a willing spirit aren't enough

Check out your local community college. Some sixteen hundred community colleges and branches are around the country, and about 16 percent of students enrolled in them are forty or over. The coursework is practical, and tuition is well below that of public universities.

to get a fulfilling job, whether it's a volunteer position or a paid one. A smart investment is to network at nonprofit organizations long before you quit your job. Otherwise, you might get stuck with boring tasks that don't take advantage of your talents.

This came home to me during a conversation with Jake Warner. Besides founding Nolo, he wrote a remarkable book about retirement, *Get a Life: You Don't Need a Million to Retire Well.* (I strongly recommend it for people thinking about what kind of life they'd like to lead now and in their old age.) "Let's say someone thinks of themselves as an environmentalist, subscribes to environmental magazines, and dreams about working in environmental causes when they retire," he said. But because of work, saving money, raising kids, all the pressures of daily life, they don't get engaged. That's for tomorrow, right?

Now they're seventy years old, and they have time. They head toward an environmental organization they admire and say, "Here I am. How can I help you?" "The answer is going to be, 'Probably not much,'" says Warner. "Now, take that same person who in their forties or fifties gets involved with several local environmental groups and at age seventy is a respected senior person. They're valued and they're needed. They earned it."

Warner illustrated the insight with the experience of his friend Afton Crooks. She was born in 1925, grew up in Seattle, and graduated from the University of Washington. She went on to become one of the first women executives in California's sprawling network of state universities. She retired in 1990 at nearly sixty-five years of age to spend more time with her husband, who had health problems. The next couple of years were rough. The wildfire that swept the Oakland hills burned down their home a year later, and her husband died the following year. She reached out to friends, gardened to connect with the earth, and worked to reach an equitable insurance settlement for the loss of her home. What would she do with her time during retirement? The first speech Crooks gave on the environment was around 1950, when the governor of Washington wanted to log the Olympic National Park. She had been involved for a long time with a number of environmental organizations in the Bay Area. Crooks found that in her retirement she had plenty of outlets to pursue her passion, improving the environment, and use the considerable organizational skills she had acquired over a lifetime.

The Creative Impulse

We often forget how creative people are at coming up with solutions. Retirement is no different. Many retirees find that they can make significant cuts in expenses without slashing their standard of living. The retired have the time to shop for and take advantage of deals and discounts, to clip coupons and plan ahead. It's easy for them to substitute home cooking instead of a late-night dash after work to get takeout. A letter writer to the *New York Times* put it nicely: "You can get by on a lot less when you're retired, without really depriving yourself of anything important . . . If I had known earlier how much 'wealth' derives from such simple pleasures, I would have retired much sooner."

When my dad retired, one of the first things he did was walk to all the nearby locally owned businesses he had supported for years, from the garage to the pharmacy. He enjoyed doing business with local entrepreneurs. He told the owners that he had stopped working. He wondered what they could do for him since he had been a loyal customer. Every owner gave him a discount, and he continued doing business with them.

Part of being creative is a willingness to experiment. Frank and Sandie learned by trial and error. Frank had been a pharmacist in Denver. Sandie worked as an assistant in doctors' offices. They owned their home, but they had recently become empty nesters. The kids were grown-up. They were looking at another fifteen years of work before they could retire. Sandie didn't have a pension from work, and Frank would get a lump-sum payout. They calculated it would be nowhere near enough to live on for the rest of their lives. "So then we decided, well, do we care if we still work? No," says Sandie. "We just don't want to work all the time."

They sold their house, bought an RV, and started living in it full-time. "We decided that if we didn't own a house, we only needed half the income," says Frank. They put into place a plan for working longer but earning less. It wasn't easy at first, however. Their first RV was too small. They went to northern California in the summer thinking it would be cool, but it was 108 degrees the first day Frank went to work. Sandie couldn't find a job. They spent more money than they made that year, too.

Eventually, they figured it out. Frank crafted a deal with his former employer to work the winter months in its pharmacy in Yuma, Arizona. Snowbirds flock there each winter, and the chain needed help. Sandie found a job working twenty to thirty hours a week as a cashier at a craft store in Yuma. They put half of Frank's income and all of Sandie's into a savings account during those six months. They have no debts. "It's best to stay out of debt," says Frank. "We do use a credit card a little bit. There are certain bills that it's just easier if they're paid for out of the credit card automatically. But take care of those every month. You don't leave a balance and carry it over."

That strategy liberates them for the next six months. They live for three months alongside a lake in the Colorado mountains. They get their site in the park and utilities for free in exchange for maintenance work at the campsite. The other three months of the year they join other RV Care-A-Vanners on the road and build Habitat for Humanity homes. "And I expect we'll work like this for, you know, ten, fifteen years," says Frank. "I don't see any reason to not continue to do this."

The Larger Impact of Working Longer

The realization that we're going to be working when we're older is starting to influence how people look at the job when they're younger. It should, too. The financial penalty of working fewer hours and doing more of the things you love is much less than you might think with a long-term time perspective. Indeed, your standard of living will probably be the same if you work less but earn an income into your seventies, or work more and then retire at age sixty or sixty-two. "The kick-back model and the profit-maximizing model are the same over time," says Alan J. Wilensky, a Minneapolis-based attorney specializing in estate planning.

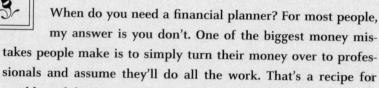

When do you need a financial planner? For most people, my answer is you don't. One of the biggest money mistakes people make is to simply turn their money over to professionals and assume they'll do all the work. That's a recipe for trouble and disappointment. You want to keep your household finances simple. It's best to do it yourself most of the time.

However, it is smart to tap into the expertise of a planner several years before a major life transition, such as retirement. You want to leave yourself enough time to plan and adjust your finances. It is helpful to talk to a knowledgeable person and get their input into your finances and circumstances. I favor fee-only planners with a certified financial planner (CFP) designation. (They charge you for their advice, but don't make a commission from selling you financial products.) They're professionals well versed in the basics of the business. They also invest in continuing education.

How to find a financial planner. Ross Levin is one of the nation's top planners. Several years ago he sent me the ABC's of the search for a planner.

A. Understand your needs: What is the triggering event that makes you feel you need a planner? Are you changing jobs, inheriting money, or do you just feel that you want more financial controls in your life?

What type of person will you feel most comfortable with discussing issues that are very personal for you? A good planner will spend a lot of time trying to understand you; you need to make sure that you are comfortable with the professional.

What would have changed in one year with your financial life if you were working successfully with a planner? Would you have drafted a will? Would you have saved tax dollars? Would you feel more comfortable with your investment philosophy?

B. "Must haves" with a planner: Your planner needs to have a certified financial planner designation. This indicates that your planner has experience, education, passed an examination, and is required to adhere to a code of ethics.

Look for a fee-based planner. While some good planners charge commissions for their services, it is usually best to pay the planner a fee directly, rather than have him or her earn a commission. There simply won't be as many conflicts of interest.

Find out if the planner's practice involves many people with situations similar to your own. Ask specifically to talk to some clients who the planner feels were in similar situations. Ask for the SEC form ADV. This tells you about a planner's philosophy, experience, and regulatory history.

Have the planners clearly lay out what they expect from the relationship. Be sure to find out what type of planning they do. Some planners give out big books filled with analysis. Other planners are more organic. You need to know what to expect.

C. Where to start: The best place to start is with your friends and colleagues. Try to be specific with what you are looking for. Ask them to be specific with you about what they like about their planner. If you have advisers who are not in the business of financial planning, ask them for recommendations. If all else fails, call the Financial Planning Association. Their phone number is 800-322-4237 and their website is fpanet.org. They will furnish you a list of planners in your area. It is still better for you to find a planner through a referral, though.

Take the experience of Tom Green. He spent half his life away from his hometown of Muncie, Indiana, logging more than seventeen thousand hours in flight time piloting commercial and corporate jets. The fifty-eight-year-old Green had planned to retire in Muncie in a couple of years when he reached his early sixties. But "retirement" came suddenly in the fall of 2008 when the major commercial real estate developer he worked for shut down its fleet of private jets. "I was forced to look at my options," says Green. "I guessed that my career was over and I'd better concentrate on a new one, just a bit earlier than I expected."

During his travels, Green had toyed with different ideas about what kind of work he might do next, in addition to trout fishing, hunting, and driving cross-country. He'd thought about owning a restaurant in Muncie. He tapped his savings and bought the Blue Bottle, a downtown coffee shop and restaurant. It's nestled in a mix of two- and three-story Victorian-era commercial buildings, some lovingly restored, others empty and waiting for rehabilitation. A group of creative entrepreneurs has moved into the historic buildings, including an upscale restaurant, a skateboarding store, and a high-tech bike shop. He's earning one-sixth of what he used to make. "But I think I can work for a long time in this job," says Green.

The longer he works, the less the blow to his income. His transition was helped by his owning his home free and clear.

In some cases, a working spouse is the savings support system. Hall Kirkham had a high-powered career, including eleven years at Cambridge Associates, a Boston consultancy that advises nonprofits on managing their endowments. Kirkham loved his job, made a good income, and met his wife there. "But I felt called to do something more," he says.

He eventually heeded the call and in 2005 entered the Episcopal Divinity School in Cambridge, Massachusetts, at age forty-one. Kirkham is now a parish priest and assistant rector at an Episcopal church in Weston, Massachusetts. His total compensation has plunged by 80 to 85 percent. The blow to his and his wife's standard of living has, however, been cushioned by her salary at Cambridge Associates. He's on her health care plan. The Episcopal Church has a good pension plan, and he should know since it was a client of his previous employer. What's more, Hall and his wife had lived frugally for years since they decided to pay off their mortgage early.

My advice is for everyone to really think about what you want to do. Then play with the numbers. You can do it yourself, use an online financial-planning program, or hire a financial planner to come up with a blueprint for you. Here's a simulation Professor Kotlikoff ran for me. We came up with a fake family and financial situation to illustrate the trade-off between a high salary and retiring early and a lower salary and working longer. Like all simulations, it's a bit unrealistic. But it gives you an idea of what to think about.

Janet is a fifty-five-year-old heart surgeon earning $250,000 a year. She is burned-out. Her husband, Jack, is also fifty-five. He is now unemployed and has a modest earnings history. Their sixteen-year-old son will head off to college in three years. Kotlikoff built many assumptions into his model, from college costs to property taxes. Among the more critical figures are $500,000 in a 401(k), another $500,000 in assets, and $100,000 left on a mortgage. They'll take Social Security at age seventy. Kotlikoff assumes a 3 percent inflation rate, a 6 percent return on retirement assets, and a 5 percent return on taxable assets.

Here's how the numbers could work: Janet quits her high-powered job for one that pays $65,300 a year. It's work that she loves. She offsets the big drop in income by tapping into the family's taxable savings. Janet continues to save some money in a 401(k). She works until she's seventy-five. Her family's standard of living would stay the same as if she had remained at her $250,000 job and retired at age sixty. If she decided to kick back at seventy, a salary of $73,250 would maintain her family's standard of living. If Janet chooses to retire at sixty-five, the same story holds at $113,555.

When you do a comparable exercise, are you coming up short financially? What would it take to fund a shift in a career? What are the risks? What is your margin of safety? How can the values of sustainability support your decision? These questions are worth asking and figuring out the answers.

Will You Have Enough?

How does anyone figure if he or she has saved enough for old age? Even people who follow the markets, page through investing books, and confer with their money advisers are haunted by financial uncertainty and wonder whether they have really set aside enough for life's later stages. The short answer is you can't know. No magic number, no infallible rule of thumb solves the "How much savings do I need in old age?" equation.

However, this isn't a brief for money despair and financial-planning nihilism. Quite the contrary. To be sure, the professionals differ on how much you can safely withdraw from your retirement savings every year without running out of money. A reasonable rule of thumb is to begin with annual withdrawals at 3 percent to 4 percent of your portfolio. That figure is then adjusted in subsequent years to take inflation into account. But that's just a starting point.

I have three strong cautions to that conventional perspective. First, many of our common images of our retirement years are wrong. There is a sense that we'll be doing less and spending less. Yet in many cases that's far from the truth, especially if you're healthy. We're curious, we're active, and we're very aware that we only go around once. Second, I would start drawing on savings very cautiously at first. There is always a big gap between a financial plan—no matter how well designed and thought through—and the reality of everyday existence. You might be better off than you anticipated or burning through more cash than you planned on. You want to leave yourself a margin of safety to make adjustments to your finances. Last, I would enter retirement debt free. It's liberating.

Still, the combination of sustainable frugality and a margin of safety from savings will be adequate for most people. We'll adjust our spending and expenses as we go along. People are already making remarkable progress reducing their debts in a relatively short time. We'll work longer, too.

The returns on getting started early are enormous, and not only because savings compound with time, as do the financial and environ-

Financial planning tools

There is no shortage of financial planning software and online tools. I like two in particular. Both offer a mix of free and fee planning tools, as well as articles and other sources of helpful information. They're very different in orientation.

analyzenow.com. Savings is the core of Henry "Bud" Hebeler's outlook on planning. His retirement programs are good, and he offers users the option of simple planners that are free, to more complete and complicated ones that come with a modest charge. Hebeler's Social Security calculators are among the best in the business. It's the place to go if you want to think through the trade-offs of taking Social Security at sixty-two, your full retirement age (sixty-six for those born between 1943 and 1954), or waiting until age seventy. You should also check out his book, *Getting Started in a Financially Secure Retirement.*

esplanner.com. Boston University economics professor Laurence Kotlikoff is also head of ESPlanner. Kotlikoff puts spending at the center of his planning programs. He has a basic plan for free that takes into account many aspects of our finances, including federal and state taxes and Social Security. The centerpiece program the firm charges for is dense, time-consuming, and requires lots of data. It also spews out a lot of interesting analysis and suggestions. He lays out his personal-finance ideas in a book coauthored with Scott Burns, *Spend 'Til the End: The Revolutionary Guide to Raising Your Living Standard, Today and When You Retire.*

mental gains from sustainable frugality. No, there's no reason to hold off figuring out what counts. What are you waiting for? I learned that lesson the hard way on May 21, 2007. I was out in Los Angeles visiting *Marketplace.* I was about to go into a taping session when I noticed I had a voice mail on my cell phone. "Please call me back," said the doctor who'd

For many retirees, adding an immediate annuity to their investment mix often makes sense. You get a predictable monthly income (or quarterly or annually depending on which payout option you chose) on the money for the rest of your life. An immediate annuity offers financial peace of mind. However, to maintain some financial flexibility you don't want to annuitize all your savings.

That said, there are a number of factors to consider. You should only do business with a highly rated blue chip financial services company. You'll need to shop around since your stream of income depends on how much you invest, your age, the interest rate, and other factors. If you're married, I recommend a payout guaranteed to last as long as each partner lives. That means a smaller payout than an immediate annuity based solely on one life.

Inflation is another critical factor. After all, what's one of the biggest risks facing retirees and their savings? It's inflation. Think about it: One hundred dollars loses half its value in twenty years with a 3.5 percent average annual rate of inflation. The same sum falls by about a third over two decades even at a modest 2 percent inflation rate. Again, you'll take a lower payout from the annuity in exchange for inflation protection, but it can be worth it. "I like inflation-protected immediate annuities," says Bud Hebeler. "I bought mine years ago, and it has a 10 percent inflation cap. Imagine what that inflation protection is worth if we go through President Carter–like inflation."

performed my colonoscopy. No information. No cheery "Everything's okay." This isn't good, I thought. I called him and found out I had colon cancer. *Cancer* is such an ominous word. A bit numb, I went and did my radio taping.

A small part of my colon was surgically removed. I went through six months of chemo. Cancer is emotionally draining and financially expensive. It was also wonderful. That sounds strange, but it was moving how family and friends rallied around offering unconditional love. Colleagues couldn't have been more supportive. Cancer was a wake-up call. One of the cards I got had this message from Lewis Carroll's *Through the Looking Glass.* "There is no use trying," said Alice; "one can't believe impossible things." "I dare say you haven't had much practice," said the Queen. "When I was your age, I always did it for half an hour a day. Why, sometimes I've believed as many as six impossible things before breakfast."

The conversation about money and life in this book started during a chemo session. My hope is to encourage you to think about what you want to do with your life and to offer up practical tools to get there. It's a never-ending question. But that's the fun in it.

CHAPTER 9

Home, Sweet Home

Ah! There is nothing like staying at home for real comfort.
—Jane Austen

A HOME, A PLACE TO CALL YOUR OWN, has long symbolized the American Dream. But is a home still worth owning following the collapse of one of the biggest bubbles in history—residential real estate?

The wrong takeaway is that home ownership is a mistake. Owning still makes sense for many of us. The right lesson is to ignore the two biggest lies in the real estate business (and there are many contenders for a spot on that list). The first lie is to "buy as much home as you can." It's a recipe for financial trouble. The second lie is renting is "throwing your money away." It's wrong.

The real question is, which offers you a better margin of safety when you are in the market for shelter, owning or renting?

Price and Savings Matter

It's an all-too-familiar story told to *Marketplace Money* host Tess Vigeland in 2007. Monique Parker is well educated with a degree in history from UCLA and half of two master's degrees. She had good job earning about $80,000 a year. Homes are expensive in southern California, and she could never quite pull enough together to buy a house. That is, until 2003, when banks abandoned traditional lending guidelines. She got a $400,000 mortgage on a house in Long Beach, California. Her credit report was spotty, so the mortgage was an interest-only, adjustable-rate loan—a classic subprime loan. Two years later she refinanced into another subprime loan. But Parker had borrowed too much, and she lost the house two years later. Her stake in the American Dream, she said, "turned out to be a nightmare."

The same can't be said for the Gilberts. Jamillah, her husband, Mark, and their four children live in an integrated, blue-collar neighborhood in Bloomington, Illinois. It's 150 miles south of Chicago and almost 2,000 miles from Long Beach. The Gilberts' home is small—a two-story, two-bedroom, one-bathroom house. They've lived there for twelve years. The three girls share a room, and the son sleeps on a mattress in the upstairs hall. Mark and Jamillah are special-education teachers at a local public high school. Jamillah teaches students with emotional disturbances and mental illnesses. The small home allowed them to spend on their children's education and to save money.

Jamillah took a remarkable journey to get here. In the early seventies, when she was five, her family lived in a public-housing project on Chicago's west side. The projects were deteriorating. Valencia Morris, Jamillah's mother, got her family out by taking advantage of a Chicago reform program that moved low-income African-American families into neighboring white suburbs. She and her three young daughters moved twenty miles west of Chicago, to Woodridge. It was a very different world. Jamillah recalls meeting one biracial girl her age. Everyone else was white. Valencia Morris worked two jobs, earned a nursing degree, and got off welfare. Her three daughters were awarded full scholarships to the University of Illinois and went on to professional careers.

When radio producer Laurie Stern and I met the Gilberts, they were looking to move to a bigger house. The previous day the mother and girls had toured various homes for sale in Bloomington and Normal, an adjacent town. Nia Gilbert, a charming nine-year-old daughter, painted a picture of the home she wanted: "I would like to see my own room. I would like to see a big kitchen, or a midsized kitchen. I would like to see a medium-sized dining room. I would like to see a big living room. I would like to see my family be very happy in that house." The Gilberts had savings and the equity in their home. They bought a bigger home in nearby Normal. They still have a margin of financial safety.

Home Economics

What's the outlook for the housing market? My sense is that the job and income health of a region will reassert their power over local real estate prices. The ebb and flow of home values will largely be dependent on local conditions. In the words of a 2009 *BusinessWeek* story on the housing market, it will be "back to blissful boredom."

It would be a welcome respite. It has been a long time since the market has been boring. In the late 1980s, the widespread belief was that home prices were in for a long period of decline, after taking inflation into account. America's demographic profile suggested that too many aging baby boomers would find too few young home buyers for their homes. David Weil and Gregory Mankiw, both economists at Harvard University back then, famously forecast that demographics would drive real housing prices down by some 47 percent, or 3 percent a year between 1987 and 2007. "Even if the fall in housing prices is only one-half what our equation predicts, it will likely be one of the major economic events of the next two decades," they wrote. (Of course, considering the carnage in the real estate market since 2007, perhaps they were just off by a couple of years?)

Instead, home prices rose by an inflation-adjusted 67 percent during those two decades. Even more stunning, real home prices surged 86 percent from the residential real estate market's bottom in 1996 to its peak in 2006. A number of factors sent the market soaring. Among the most important were falling interest rates, immigrant homebuyers, single women with good incomes putting down stakes, and baby boomers trading up.

Eventually, spiraling prices helped stoke a mass mania, and real estate speculation spun out of control. And, as we all know, in 2007 the bubble burst with catastrophic economic consequences.

So, let's take a step away from the housing market's peaks and valleys. Fact is, homeownership isn't a good investment. It never has been, and it never will be no matter what real estate agents say. Yes, I know all the stories about people making vast sums of money off their houses. A home offers plenty of tax benefits, including the deductibility of mortgage interest payments and no capital taxes due on home sale gains under half a million dollars (for joint filers). But those gains are offset by the price of ownership, including mortgage interest payments and property taxes. The cost of maintenance is steep. So is the price tag on any improvements you make to a home. Data going back to the 1850s suggests the long-term after-inflation return of real estate is about 2.5 to 3 percent, calculates economist Karl Case of Wellesley College. His close academic colleague and business partner, Yale University finance professor Robert Shiller, figures even that modest return is too high. He argues that the return on residential real estate over the past one hundred years has been zero. That's right: zero.

I think the low-return numbers on home ownership are right. Nevertheless, owning isn't a mistake for many people. For one thing, you automatically increase your savings as you pay down your mortgage. Even more important, a home is a lifestyle. It's a place where you live with all the psychological and emotional benefits that come with decorating and landscaping it the way you want. "This is the true nature of home," said nineteenth-century art critic John Ruskin. "It is the place of Peace; the shelter, not only from injury, but from all terror, doubt, and division."

My principal guidelines to weighing the costs and benefits of home-ownership are:

- Compare the cost of owning versus renting. Either one is good, depending on the numbers.

- Buy only if the deal is financially conservative.

- Keep the financing simple.

- Smaller is both financially smart and socially sustainable.

A home is the most expensive and complicated investment we make. Ownership can offer a wonderful lifestyle if it's financed with a margin of safety. It's potentially disastrous for people who stretch their finances to buy.

Rent-versus-Own Equation

Number crunching helps keep emotions in check. The rental and ownership markets compete for your money. Let's say you calculate that the monthly cost of ownership, taking tax benefits into consideration, is significantly higher than the monthly price of renting for a comparable property. If you buy a home, you're making a bet that home prices will rise to justify the purchase. But you have a financial cushion if the cost of ownership is closer to rental values.

The price-to-rent ratio is one way to calculate how expensive homes are relative to rentals. It's essentially the same idea as the price-to-earnings ratio for stocks. The P/E ratio comes from dividing a company's stock price by its earnings per share. A high P/E ratio means investors are optimistic about a company's prospects. They're willing to pay a high price for the stock. You can't take the ratio too literally, but it's a quick way to gauge how expensive or cheap a stock price is relative to a company's earnings history.

The price-to-rent ratio is simply the value of a home divided by annual rent. A low P/R ratio suggests there's value in ownership, a high P/R ratio indicates that the market is overvalued. The long run P/R ratio is about 16, according to economist Mark Zandi of Moody's Economy.com. In the 1990s the national P/R ratio was in the 14 to 15 range, he calculated for *Fortune* in 2007. In the 2000s, the article notes that the ratio jumped to 24, an increase of 60 percent. The P/R figures were even higher than that in the bubble markets on the two coasts.

You'll want to check out the P/R ratio in your area. In the spring of 2009 I looked into my area in the Twin Cities. A two-bedroom, one-bath rental with nice amenities was on the market for $1,000 a month. The annual rent cost was $12,000. In the same neighborhood a two-bedroom, one-bath condo was for sale in the $250,000 range. The P/R ratio was about 21. That's above the fifteen-year average of some 15.5. Home prices still seemed high relative to rents in my area.

The P/R ratio, like the P/E ratio, is only an indication. You need to delve into more detail. Online calculators will do the math for you. There are a number of good ones, but I tend to gravitate toward the Web sites www.dinkytown.net and www.hsh.com. What goes into rent? There is your security deposit, the monthly rent payment, and any anticipated rent increases. You'll also need to make a guesstimate of how much you might make if you invested your closing costs and down payment instead of purchasing a home. The homeownership side of the equation includes the price of the home, the mortgage rate, the down payment, closing costs, maintenance and taxes, tax rate, insurance costs, how long you expect to live in the home, the anticipated appreciation of your investment, and several other factors. I would take the time to play with the numbers and run a range of scenarios.

Let's go back to the rental and condo in my neighborhood. I'll put 20 percent down. I'll get a thirty-year, fixed-rate mortgage at 6 percent. My monthly payment will be $1,922 (consisting of principal, interest, taxes, insurance, and association and maintenance dues). I'm in the 28 percent tax bracket. I'll assume that the condo will appreciate 2.5 percent a year. I'll assume that my investments will grow at 2.5 percent annually. Inflation will average 2 percent. After I take into account closing costs, commission costs, and a number of other expenses, my home purchase doesn't break even for eleven years compared to renting. If I made a 10 percent down payment and kept everything else the same, it would take me about fifteen years to reach the break-even point. But with 20 percent down and a 5 percent mortgage rate, the break-even figure drops to less than seven years.

Time is critical. The longer you intend to stay in a home, the better the financial advantages of ownership. It's safe to say that if you plan on staying in a place for three years or less, renting is always preferable. Ownership really doesn't make sense unless you're confident that your time horizon is at least five years, and preferably longer.

Renting can make financial sense even if the numbers are close, especially if you save. The key from a financial perspective is to set up an automatic savings program. This way you'll build up savings over the years. It's important to realize that you can have many of the amenities of homeownership as a renter, from a nice kitchen to a good community. It's why Michelle and Ted Redmond of Minneapolis rent. They and their daughter, Rachel, live in a two-bedroom apartment in a turn-of-the-century complex. "It provides us with the opportunity to have a more simplified living style," says Ted Redmond. "If there's a maintenance problem, we just call up the management company and they come and fix it."

Conservative Financing

Small is beautiful. It's both financially practical and environmentally sustainable to own a smaller home rather than a bigger one. It's easier to come up with a large down payment with a smaller home. The mortgage is less, too. So are insurance, taxes, and heating and cooling bills. These cost savings compound over time. This approach is also friendlier to the environment.

The surge in foreclosures in recent years underlined the risks in stretching your finances to buy. Homeownership is expensive even in less tumultuous times. It's not just the mortgage, taxes, and insurance costs. It takes money to maintain a home. When you move in, you'll see that the furniture you've accumulated while renting looks wrong. That's an additional expense. You may be excited about finally having a garden to tend, but that

Homeowner insurance varies a lot

The terms are confusing. Don't skimp on the time you spend shopping around and learning what your policy covers. The Insurance Information Institute, an industry trade group, offers the basics at www.iii.org. (It's a good resource for learning about all kinds of insurance.)

Most insurance policies will cover replacement cost for damage to the structure. It pays for the repair and replacement of damaged property with similar materials. An extended replacement-cost policy pays an extra 20 percent or more above your policy limits. The best policy is a guaranteed replacement-cost policy. It will pay whatever it costs to rebuild your home. It's more expensive and harder to find.

If it's an older home, you might have to buy a modified replacement-cost policy. The insurance company doesn't want to pay for replacing those beautiful antique floors and molded tin ceiling. The policy will use contemporary building materials.

Inflation protection costs more, but it adjusts the policy limit to reflect changes in construction costs in your area.

You should do a home inventory to learn the value of what you own. You should also keep a record by videotaping every room in your house. The policy typically covers about 50 to 70 percent of the amount of insurance you have on your home. You'll need to decide whether to insure your belongings for their cash value or their replacement cost. The Insurance Information Institute uses this example to illustrate the difference: A fire destroys your ten-year-old TV in your living room. If you have a replacement-cost policy, the insurer will pay to replace the TV set with a new one. If you have a cash-value policy, it pays only a percentage of the cost of a new TV set. It isn't worth much. You can increase your coverage for certain expensive items, such as jewelry.

Check carefully to see how much the insurance company will cover if you have to move out of the home because of a disaster.

Liability coverage protects you against lawsuits for bodily injury or property damage that you or family members cause to other people. A minimum for many homeowners is buying at least $300,000 to $500,000 worth of liability coverage.

DATA: Insurance Information Institute

pleasure costs money. At the same time, you're trying to accumulate an emergency fund and set money aside for your retirement. This is why my basic message is so conservative.

No one likes paying private mortgage insurance. An alternative is the 80-10-10 peddled in the 2000s. Here's the basic idea: You take out a mortgage worth 80 percent of the purchase price (and pay fees). You then borrow another 10 percent with a second mortgage at a higher interest rate (and pay fees for that loan). The remaining 10 percent is your down payment. Still, you have a 20 percent down payment and no PMI requirement. The money you borrowed is tax-deductible. Problem is, the interest rate on the second mortgage is almost always an adjustable-rate loan that can rise when the market changes. It typically charges a rate about 2 percentage points higher than your primary mortgage. It encouraged homeowners to take on too big a debt burden and buy too much house. It's a less common technique after the bubble burst. But it will return, and it should be avoided.

The size of the down payment is critical. The traditional guideline of a 20 percent down payment or more is still best. A 10 percent down payment is the minimum. I'd forget about owning if you can't put at least 10 percent down. In the 2000s too many people put less than 10 percent down—sometimes as little as nothing—and ended up in financial trouble. Many of them eventually lost their home. Lenders will require you to take out private mortgage insurance (PMI) if your equity stake is under 20 percent. It protects the lender somewhat against the cost of your defaulting on the loan. You can cancel your PMI once the equity in your home is at 20 percent.

You will be surprised how much lenders are willing to let you borrow. The standard financial-institution ratio on how much debt you can take on is that no more than 28 percent of your income should go toward the mortgage, and that includes principal, interest, taxes, and insurance. A broader rule of thumb is no more than 36 percent of your income should go to your mortgage (principal, interest, taxes, and insurance) and all other debts, including car loans and student loans. I'd recommend backing off those figures slightly.

 ### *How many points do you want to pay?*

A point equals 1 percent of the loan amount. One point on a $100,000 loan is $1,000. The more points you pay your lender at closing, the lower your interest rate. Lenders offer all kinds of point and interest-rate combinations. If you expect to move at some point out of the house, it may make sense to get a no-point or one-point mortgage. But if this is the house of your dreams, you may want to pay several points to lock in a lower interest rate. No-point loans are popular when interest rates are high because the borrower expects to refinance the loan at a later date when interest rates come down.

Mortgages are complicated. So, let's keep it simple. Only three mortgage choices are sensible for most people. You can easily comparison shop all three. You don't want any prepayment penalty. You don't want any hidden fees. You don't want negative amortization.

The thirty-year, fixed-rate mortgage: You know what your monthly payments will be for the life of the loan. The interest rate won't change. It makes financial planning easier. It comes with a higher interest rate than other choices, but the extra interest cost is well worth the certainty of the payment. You can refinance if rates go lower.

The fifteen-year, fixed-rate mortgage: It saves you a lot in interest payments. For example, a $100,000 mortgage at 6.25 percent for thirty years will cost you about $121,650 in interest if your marginal tax rate is 25 percent. The interest charge on a fifteen-year mortgage at 6 percent is $51,900. (The rate on a fifteen-year mortgage is lower than the thirty-year rate.) It's a good move if you have the cash flow to absorb the higher monthly mortgage tab.

The 5/25 and the 7/23: These are adjustable-rate mortgages that offer

---

The thirteenth monthly payment

Another option for accelerating mortgage payments is to borrow at a thirty-year fixed rate, locking in the lower monthly outlay. At some point during the year, you make an extra monthly payment. You cut your interest payments significantly this way. For instance, by making one more monthly payment on a $100,00 thirty-year, fixed-rate mortgage at 6.25 percent, you'll shorten the life of the loan by five years, saving almost $26,000 in interest. The advantage of this approach is flexibility. Let's say your financial circumstances change—you lose your job, you need a new car, your children need extra tutoring—you can always go back to the thirty-year payment schedule with no penalty.

some of the security of a conventional mortgage for the first few years. For instance, with the 7/23 the interest rate is fixed for the first seven years, then it floats for the remainder of the 30-year loan. You'll need to understand how the interest rate adjustment works. What is the underlying index? Common interest-rate benchmarks include one-year and three-year Treasury securities. How much can the interest rate move up and down in a year, and how high can it go in a worst-case scenario? It's a riskier loan than the conventional fixed rate mortgage.

As with any financial product, it pays to compare closing costs and loan-processing fees. You want to keep all your upfront fees as low as possible.

Shared Equity

When home prices soared into the stratosphere in the 2000s, many young adults and longtime renters took on too much debt to buy. Prices have come down a lot since then. Still, it can be tough to come up with the kind of conservative financing structure I'm recommending.

It isn't for everyone, but investing in a home with family is worth exploring. A growing number of "sandwich generation" families—responsible for taking care of aging parents and young children—are embracing a living arrangement common a few generations ago. "It offers less expensive independent living for older people, and it's very good from a family perspective," says Elinor Ginzler, director of livable communities at AARP.

Paul Royal agrees. He wasn't thinking about his parents when he and his wife, Bonnie, decided to move into Exeter, New Hampshire, from its rural outskirts. They had in mind their son, Andrew, then two. They felt he would benefit from having nearby neighbors.

While they were house hunting, they saw a for-sale sign for the "House of the Future." Intrigued, they checked it out. The custom-built home was really two dwellings under one roof: a twenty-four-hundred-square-foot single-family unit with a fourteen-hundred-square-foot mother-in-law apartment in the basement. Each part of the house had its own entrance, kitchen, laundry room, and garage space. Paul realized the setup was perfect for his family and his elderly parents. They lived ninety miles away, and he was getting tired of the long weekly drive to see them. With everyone under the same roof, he and his wife would be there in case of an accident or a health problem with his parents. His son would grow closer to his grandparents. The separate apartment allowed for privacy. "It's such a great solution for us," says Paul, a forty-four-year-old financial planner.

That said, the move represented a big financial and emotional commitment for an extended family. It involved many hours devising financial plans that worked for all parties. His two sisters lived in different states, and it was important that they agreed with the arrangement. Perhaps most difficult were the many hours of frank discussion about disability and death. What were his parents' wishes if one of them died? What if Mom or Dad ended up in a nursing home? "You have to really think about the endgame, more than a lot of people are comfortable doing," says Paul.

Family members don't have to live in the same dwelling to share equity. It's more common for parents to help out as investors. David Ragan and his wife, Jocelyn, turned to his father as an equity investor in their new home. "We have a lot of older clients who say they're interested in helping out their kids," says Jared Roskelley, a certified financial planner in Scottsdale, Arizona. "And the kids tell us they're interested in getting help from their parents."

Check on your local regulations if you're creating a multigenerational household. Zoning restrictions often prohibit converting a garage into living space, building a backyard cottage, or adding a separate apartment in a neighborhood of single-family residences. A number of communities are modifying their zoning laws to encourage such dwellings, however. The AARP is pushing model legislation in jurisdictions around the country.

The Ragans were living in a starter home they had bought for $125,000 in a rural area outside Denton, Texas. Since then, their family had expanded with two children. The Ragans wanted to live in a bigger home in a more established neighborhood in Denton with good schools. At the time we talked, a house like that would go for $180,000 to $200,000. It would be a stretch for their finances. Instead, Ragan worked out a deal with his father. His father put $50,000 into the down payment. The Ragans added to it from the sale of their home. The equity sharing allowed the couple to purchase a larger home and keep their finances conservative. His father gets his investment back plus a share of the appreciation. In a $200,000 home, his $50,000 investment gets him 25 percent of the gain. "This allows my family to live in a better neighborhood that we could not have otherwise afforded," says Ragan. "It allows my father to participate in real estate appreciation without going out and purchasing something himself."

The Ragans struck a typical deal. Investors, usually parents, put in enough cash so that their child has at least a 20 percent down payment. The young homeowner qualifies for a conventional thirty-year, fixed-rate mortgage. The investors get back their initial stake plus 10 percent to 50 percent of the profits when the home is sold. But these deals are extremely flexible and everything is up for negotiation. It's critical that lawyers represent both parties, and that a written contract spells out the terms. A lawyer will help family members avoid letting their emotions cloud their financial judgment. The price of love can be steep. Jared Roskelley tells this warning story. A sixty-year-old divorcée was living on her investment income. She gave her daughter $40,000 as a down payment for a first home. The mother expected that she would get back the $40,000 plus 20 percent of the profit when the home was sold. But the agreement wasn't in writing. A few years later the daughter sold the home, but instead of repaying her mother, she loaned the money to her boyfriend, who was starting a business. The relationship went bust. So did his business. No money was recovered.

At the moment, shared-equity financings are largely ad hoc legal agreements negotiated between well-off parents and their young-adult children. A couple of companies are offering homeowners shared-equity deals with outside investors, but so far it appears many people will do better taking out a traditional loan–or waiting longer to buy. In the meantime, families may find it advantageous for everyone to negotiate their own deals. Done right, it's an example of win-win financing.

CHAPTER 10

The College Sheepskin

Stay Hungry. Stay Foolish.
                              —Whole Earth Catalog

ALL RIGHT, TAKE OUT YOUR NO. 2 PENCILS.

When it comes to a college education:
   a. A record number of young adults are applying
   b. Only half of undergraduates get their degree in six years
   c. Both of the above

Students are borrowing more to pay for college because:
   a. College costs have risen more than four times the rate of inflation for over two decades
   b. Family incomes have stagnated
   c. Both of the above

College graduates earn:
   a. About $16,000 more a year than their high-school-degree-only peers

b. Wages that barely beat the rate of inflation over the past decade

c. Both of the above

Go to the head of the class if you answered *c* to all three questions.

A college degree is a passport to better earnings and more employment over a lifetime. Employers want educated workers. College graduates are more likely to get jobs with health insurance and an employer-sponsored pension. The median college graduate earns considerably more than his or her peers who stopped their education with a high school diploma. "For many people, it's the most valuable investment they are going to make," says Michael McPherson, former dean of Macalester College and now head of the Spencer Foundation, a Chicago-based education institute. "I think students come out of college as better citizens, as more thoughtful members of their communities, maybe with

---

Education pays

	MEDIAN ANNUAL EARNINGS AGES 25–34, FULL-TIME, FULL-YEAR WORKERS
Master's degree or higher	$56,000
Bachelor's degree	45,000
Associate degree	35,000
Some college, no degree	33,000
High school graduate	29,000
Less than a high school diploma	23,000

DATA: U.S. Department of Education, 2007

different cultural tastes and cultural tendencies than they would have otherwise."

McPherson's outlook on a college degree is widely shared, including by Donna Kelly and Jerry Miranowski. They put a big value on a college education. He's an attorney. She had worked as director of a gift at Macalester that went toward neighborhood and community relations. She left that job to spend more time with her two children in their last years of high school. She earned a degree in career and life counseling. Both their kids went to Middlebury College. Their children weren't going to inherit money and an estate. Their legacy was an education. "It's what we spend all our discretionary income on—education," Kelly said. "We look on it as an investment in their lives, not necessarily a return on their careers. It's an investment in their life skills."

I couldn't agree more. A major factor behind the embrace of a college degree and graduate-school education is that the wealth of the nation increasingly relies on knowledge, skill, and education—the endowments economists call human capital. Its worth to the economy is three to four times greater than the value of all stocks, all bonds, all real estate, and all other assets, estimates Professor Gary Becker, Nobel laureate at the University of Chicago. Ralph Waldo Emerson was right when he wrote, "Wealth is mental; wealth is moral."

Almost all the job growth in the economy in the past several decades has been in professions, careers, and jobs that require at least some college experience. For instance, over the past decade much of the growth in employment has been in health care and education. Job growth in these two sectors held up even during the Great Recession. Management, supervision, coordination, and planning-type jobs are also strong, and the jobs in these areas require a higher education degree to break in. The work of business, government, and nonprofits is increasingly complicated and demanding. It's striking how jobs that were once filled by high school graduates now often require a two-year associate degree or a certificate of accomplishment from a community college.

Globalization, an abstruse word for describing the strengthening links between countries, enhances the economic value of a college education.

Universities are in the vanguard of a global human-capital revolution. Some 20 percent of the world's young adults are participating in higher education. To put that figure in perspective, Algeria, Kazakhstan, and Myanmar each has as many students enrolled in higher education as the entire world did at the start of the twentieth century. A college education makes it easier for business, government, and community leaders from around the world to carry on conversations with one another. Universities in the United States, Germany, Brazil, Iran, China, and elsewhere promote similar standards of reason and rationality. It also means that the competition for knowledge jobs is intense.

Cost Is Important

In the twenty-first century a college sheepskin is key to gaining access to the American Dream. And that concerns me. There's no question in my mind about the value of a college degree for young people. The worry is the price paid for that diploma. Price matters, whether it's in buying a stock, a home, or a college degree. For instance, a home was long the symbol of the American Dream. The giant real-estate-and-lending complex fed the notion that you could never borrow too much to own. A home always paid off. But home values did plummet during the Great Recession. Many folks learned that they had borrowed more than their stagnant incomes justified.

Similarly, the college-and-student-lending complex assures everyone that a college education is worth it. For more than three decades, students and their parents have funded a college-tuition bubble, largely with borrowed money. An ample supply of loans allowed colleges to raise their bills at four times the rate of inflation over the past two decades. Total federal student loans swelled by 70 percent from 1997–1998 to 2007–2008, according to the College Board. The number of borrowers maxing out on their student loans surged from 57 percent to 73 percent at the same time.

For young college graduates, student-loan-debt burdens are the main fi-

Be wary of credit cards for students

The law now says that students under twenty-one years of age can't get a credit card unless their parents or guardian cosigns or they can prove their ability to pay. The credit limit on a card is capped to the greater of $500 or 20 percent of their annual income unless there is a cosigner. It's a good law. Many universities and colleges wrongly gave credit card companies access to their students for a fee. Nellie Mae, the nonprofit student lender, reports that 76 percent of undergraduates had a credit card, and that the median debt was just under $1,000. It's all too easy for undergraduates to get into a debt hole with credit cards. Debit cards are much better.

nancial worry. Recent research explodes, too, the widespread myth that student loan default rates are low. The U.S. Department of Education has said for years that the default rate was a relatively modest 4 to 5 percent. Yet the federal agency only looks at the first two years of debt repayments. Longer-term studies find far more dire results. For instance, reaching back into the 1990s and following students over the subsequent decade, students with loans totaling $15,000 or more had nearly triple the default rate of those with $5,000 or less in loans—19 percent versus 7 percent. For African-American students with large debts the default rate is almost 40 percent—an outrageous figure. It's likely the default rates are much higher now since debt burdens are much larger than in the early nineties.

The student-loan-debt burden is real. From 1982 to 2007, the cost of fees and tuition surged by 439 percent. Yet median family income increased only 147 percent, according to the nonprofit research organization the National Center for Public Policy and Higher Education. Young college graduates (ages 25–34) aren't getting the kind of wage increases that make it easy to pay off large debts. From 1997 to 2007 the real median wages of young college graduates with a bachelor's degree only increased a mere 1.6 percent, according to calculations by Michael Mandel, chief economist at *BusinessWeek*. That's hardly a reassuring return on education for a generation that has taken on unprecedented debts. Still, while the Great Recession was brutal on most workers, those without a college degree were hit especially hard. "Having a college degree does not necessarily reward you," says Patrick Callan, president of the National Center for Public Policy and Higher Education. "But those who don't have degrees are relentlessly punished in this economy."

Put it this way: A college degree used to be the equivalent of owning a hot growth stock. It's more like buying an unemployment-insurance policy now. It's a smart move to get a college sheepskin.

The new face of poverty also comes with a student loan. In working on stories about poverty in Memphis, Chicago, and Muncie, it was striking how many low-income people knew a college degree was a way to a better life. Almost everyone we talked to had been to community college, junior college, a public four-year university. But for a variety of reasons—from pregnancy to lost income—they didn't get a degree. What they got were student loans. For example, low-income, first-generation students who left school during their first year owed $6,557 on average. Those leaving in their fourth year had an average of $16,548 in student loans, according to the Pell Institute. These students must pay back their loans without the extra earnings power associated with attaining a degree. You can't get rid of student loans by declaring bankruptcy.

What does all this mean for students and their parents? The wrong lesson is that college is a scam. I would ignore a fashionable stream of commentary suggesting that a college sheepskin doesn't pay. For instance, ABC's *20/20* coanchor John Stossel in early 2009 profiled Rachele Percel. She had borrowed about $24,000 a year to attend Rivier College, a Catholic liberal arts college in New Hampshire. "I was told just to take out the loans and get the degree because when you graduate, you're going to be able to get that good job and pay them off no problem," she said. Three years later she's working at a low-paying desk job. She's still $85,000 in debt. "I definitely feel like it was a scam," Rachele says about college. "Self-serving college presidents and politicians should drop the scam," says Stossel. "Higher enrollments and government loan programs may be good for them, but they are making lots of our kids miserable and poor."

Rachele's story is disturbing. But Stossel goes too far. The job, career, and financial social rewards of college are too great for most people to pass up in the global economy. Even more valuable are the intangibles, the conversation and learning that help turn us into engaged, educated citizens of the planet. My message is to borrow with, you guessed it, a margin of safety. Parents and students should carefully think through the downside and the upside of their college choices. They need to plan more and take active steps to keep the overall debt burden down. But get the degree.

A Message for Parents

It's smart to save for your children's college educations. The earlier you start, the more money you'll accumulate. Savings will limit how much you and your child will borrow for college. It allows your student to dream big, to focus on the college experience rather than the price tag.

That said, I would put college-education savings down on your list of priorities. Yes, you read that right. You need to pay yourself first, siphoning off money for everything from your emergency fund to your retirement portfolio. You should put the effort into creating a margin of safety for your household. You can always draw on those savings to help defray the cost of college. To me, college savings is simply part of the automatic savings program you've established over the years. Some of your savings is going into a savings account, and some of it into certificates of deposit and the like. You should also consider regularly investing money in a broad-based stock index fund, such as the Wilshire 5000, the Russell 3000, or the Standard & Poor's 500. You could load up on tax-deferred, inflation-protected I-bonds for the fixed-income portion of your portfolio. The mix of secure and riskier savings accumulates over time. It may be tapped to fund a career change, a medical emergency, or college tuition bills. This simple strategy gives you a lot of flexibility.

It's my favorite tactic for college savings. It combines a margin of safety and the keep-it-simple mantra.

The 529 College Savings Plan

What if you can target money for college? A tax-advantaged state-sponsored 529 college savings plan is the hands-down winner for college money. All fifty states offer 529 savings plans. Most brokers, mutual fund companies, and other financial institutions offer 529 plans.

A 529 savings plan comes with a number of advantages. You open an account for a beneficiary, your future student. The account is funded with after-tax dollars. The money grows with both federal and state taxes deferred. A majority of states and the District of Columbia allow you to deduct from state taxes some or all of your contributions. When you withdraw the accumulated earnings, it's free of federal taxes so long as it goes toward qualified educational expenses. It's usually free of state taxes. Qualified educational expenses include a wide range of bills, such as tuition, mandatory fees, books, supplies, equipment, and a personal computer.

You can own an account in any state. If you live in Minnesota and decide that you like California's 529 plan, you can open an account in the Golden State—and vice versa. The accumulated savings are available to be spent on any accredited public or private college in any state. Anyone

> Conversations about money with your students are important. Start talking to them early about the cost of college and the reality of your savings. How much can you contribute toward their education, and how much do you expect them to pay? Most teenagers don't know the price tag of college in dollars and cents. They know it's expensive. They're more than willing to help out. Listen to their ideas. Engage them in your finances.

can contribute to a 529, including parents, grandparents, uncles, aunts, cousins, and friends. A 529 plan in most states can be opened with less than $100, and the maximum is typically several hundred thousand dollars. If for some reason your child doesn't need the money to go to college, the account can always be transferred to another child or even toward your continuing education.

The federal financial-aid formula treats 529 plans favorably. (Private colleges have the leeway to consider any asset in calculating financial aid, but most follow the federal guidelines.) The plan is assessed at the parents' contribution rate of about 5.64 percent in determining the amount the family is expected to pay for college. That's far below the 20 percent contribution or more expected from the child's savings for college.

The 529 plans have drawbacks. If you take out the earnings for any reason other than paying for qualified educational expenses, you'll be hit with a 10 percent penalty and ordinary income taxes on any gain. With so many plans with all kinds of terms, it's difficult to evaluate them. Fees vary significantly, too.

To simplify your choice, it's almost always cheaper to buy a 529 plan sold directly by the state. Many of the plans sold through broker-dealers are too expensive. For instance, Minnesota's 529 plan levies a total-asset charge between 0.60 and 0.65 percent. The fee on Nebraska's AIM College Savings Plan ranges from 1.35 to 2.36 percent. (AIM is a mutual fund company.) You can put the money into a mix of fixed-income securities leavened with a slice of equities for growth.

Well-off grandparents enjoy an unusual gift benefit with 529s. Federal tax law limits gifts to $13,000 and under a year without triggering a federal gift-tax liability. However, grandparents can gift $65,000 in one year into a college savings plan and for tax purposes it's treated as if it were a $13,000 gift each year for five years (assuming no other gifts to the beneficiary).

The investment choice I prefer is a basic, plain-vanilla, age-based investment option. However, you have to be comfortable with equities. The money is invested in low-cost index funds. When your student is young, a high percentage of the portfolio—typically 70 to 80 percent—is in equities. The rest is in fixed-income securities. As your student ages, the percentage invested in equities automatically shrinks, and the amounts in bonds and cash increases. By the time the student is sixteen, equities usually comprise about a quarter or less of the portfolio. With this option you focus on savings since the asset allocation automatically shifts over time. You do need to research the different plans. In recent years, many 529 plans became aggressive with their age-based portfolios, and a number of the investment funds are actively managed. The higher-risk age-based portfolios are a bad deal. It's how many 529 savers learned to their chagrin during the bear market that their supposedly "conservative" choice actually contained a larger-than-expected exposure to stocks.

Most 529 plans now offer three age-based investment options: aggressive, moderate, and conservative. I don't see any reason to risk money in an aggressive portfolio that is heavily into stocks. Your student will go to college around age eighteen. It's a pretty inflexible date, and by the time he or she is eighteen, stocks shouldn't be in the mix. If you like the age-based option I would choose the moderate or conservative portfolio. The conservative portfolio typically shifts to all bonds and cash in the early teen years. You'll still need to look at the different plans since there is no common definition of conservative or moderate. It's also sensible to put the money into safe, fixed-income securities. You won't earn much of a

> A good Web site for researching different 529 plans is Joseph Hurley's savingforcollege.com. Hurley offers good free information. He charges for more detailed investigations. The Web site is updated to take into account changes in the law and in college savings plans.

There is another kind of state-sponsored plan. It's a "prepaid" college-tuition savings account. More than half the states offer the option. When you buy tuition "units" or "credits," you're protecting your child from future college inflation. The guarantee is attractive. However, drawbacks to prepaid plans limit their appeal. For instance, many prepaid plans have residency requirements. Most impose restrictions on where your child can attend college. If your child does go to an out-of-state school, you will get your money back, plus interest. Still, the peace of mind that comes from locking in college costs makes it an option worth investigating.

return on your money, but you'll also know how much you'll have when it's time to start paying the college tuition bill.

The 529 plan isn't the only tax-favored college-savings account. However, none of the others are as good. The Coverdell Education Savings account used to be known as the Education IRA. Like a 529, money in a Coverdell is tapped tax-free to cover qualified education expenses. However, the Coverdell savings can go toward college, primary, and secondary schools. A Coverdell can be opened at most financial institutions, which gives you a lot of investment choice. But the annual contribution limit is $2,000 until 2011, when the figure drops to $500. A number of other attractive features to the Coverdell are slated for the legislative graveyard unless Congress changes its mind. It's easier to go with the 529.

I'd also forget about saving for college in your child's name with a custodial account. Before the 529 era, well-off parents would open up a Uniform Gift to Minors Act (UGMA) or a Uniform Transfer to Minors Act (UTMA) account. These accounts allow a child or minor to own securities. The adult controls the account, but the child owns the assets. The idea was to take advantage of the child's lower tax rate when the investments were sold to pay for college. But custodial accounts are less attractive now since withdrawals are tax-free with a 529 plan and Coverdell. The other problem is that it's the kid's money. Your child takes control of the account upon reaching age eighteen or twenty-one, depending on the age of majority in your state. Although I think the problem is exaggerated, I've taken numerous calls from parents over the years regretting setting up an UGMA or UTMA. The reason is usually the same: You may have set it aside for college (a common reason), but your child may want to buy a car with it, and you can do nothing to prevent it.

Navigating Financial Aid

Let's review the numbers. At the moment, tuition and fees average about $6,600 a year for an in-state, public four-year university, $17,500 for an out-of-state, public university, and $25,000 for a private four-year college. These figures don't include room and board and lost wages while your student is in college. Add those in, and you could buy a nice home in most parts of the country. The total price tag of a four-year public university for an in-state student is more than $142,000, including tuition, fees,

> Don't be afraid of the steep price tag of a private college. Instead, negotiate. For instance, it's difficult to figure out the real cost of attending a private college. Yes, every private college publishes on its Web site the cost of attendance. The sticker price is deceiving, however. The average net price of tuition and fees for a year at a private college is $14,900, far below the average published sticker price of $25,100, according to College Board. The tactic of "tuition discounting" is widespread in higher education, but the practice is greatest with private colleges. The school may say no if you insist on a better deal after your child has been accepted. Then again, it might say yes. It's worth a try.

and lost wages. The comparable average figure for a private four-year college degree is almost \$217,000.

Those are daunting figures. What I take away from them, as I've already said, is that the lifetime return from a college education is still worth it, but the penalty for not carefully weighing the financial trade-offs in paying for that degree is steep. The risks are greater because most eighteen-year-olds don't know what they want to do when they graduate. College is a time of exploration and learning, yet that uncertainty makes it hard to judge what kind of income a student will earn after graduation. The goal is to get as good an education as possible for your student, and for your child to graduate with as little debt as possible. It's using the lens of the New Frugality to weigh the consequences of your college choices. Your student has a lifetime of earnings ahead of him or her, so taking out some loans is sensible.

Many parents and their students will have to make trade-offs. My parents always told us that they wanted us to graduate from college debt-free. It was our inheritance. After that, we were financially on our own. I feel the same way. A college education is my legacy to my sons. Their mother shares the sentiment. I rent my apartment, and while writing this book, I investigated the economics of owning. The rent-versus-buy calculation was starting to creep into the owning column. But my youngest son will be off to college soon. To maintain a household margin of safety, it was either college or buying. I wouldn't have a margin of safety if I took on both obligations. College comes first.

A good source of information about all aspects of paying for college is finaid.org. It has a free calculator for estimating the expected family contribution and financial need, and for estimating your student financial aid. Finaid is comprehensive on student and parent loans, too. Another source of information is the College Board at collegeboard.org. The U.S. Department of Education has detailed information for students and parents at ed.gov.

A number of steps can be taken to keep the price tag down. One of the simplest is to graduate in four years. The longer it takes to get your degree, the more it will end up costing you, largely because you won't enjoy the earnings benefit of a higher degree. During the Great Recession, a growing number of students transferred from out-of-state public schools or private colleges into in-state public universities. The savings from the move are large.

The basic financial-aid information sheet is the Free Application for Federal Student Aid, or Fafsa. It's a complicated form although recent initiatives are streamlining it. The financial aid system that developed in the post–World War II era was initially modeled after the U.S. progressive income tax. Over the years, like the tax code, it has evolved into a messy stew of rules. Thomas Kane is one of the nation's leading education economists, and he worked at the White House Council of Economic Advisers during the Clinton administration. The head of the council at the time was Joseph Stiglitz, a Nobel laureate and brilliant scholar. Kane recalls walking into Stiglitz's office, finding him surrounded with papers, looking extremely frustrated. What was up? A recession in the making? The details of fiscal policy? No, Stiglitz was struggling to make sense of financial aid forms for a college-bound child. "Imagine how bad it is when the process confuses someone like Stiglitz?" says Kane.

The "two-plus-two" step is an increasingly popular choice for lowering the cost of college. Your student attends a low-cost two-year community college. The annual cost of tuition and fees at a public two-year community college is around $2,400. Your student transfers to a brand-name four-year university or a private college for the final two years of his or her education. Your student's college sheepskin is from the better-known school. The diploma costs a fraction of the price paid by students who went to the college or university for the full four years.

The financial aid formula runs along these lines: You start with the yearly cost of college, including tuition, room, board, and books. You subtract the parents' and student's contribution. The parents' contribution takes into account their income and assets. The federal calculation does not include the value of your home or retirement plan. (Some private colleges do add in a fraction of what those assets are worth.) It subtracts your living expenses and taxes. Similarly, it looks at your child's income and assets. The remainder is defined as need. Need is met through a combination of scholarship, grant, loan, and work-study. It's a safe bet you'll be shocked at how much money colleges expect from you. Many middle-income families feel they're living on the financial edge and they are. It's tough to pay the monthly bills. But according to the numbers spewed out by financial aid administrators, you're living fat and easy with plenty of money to contribute.

Grants are based on the student's financial need. They don't need to be paid back. Work-study programs provide jobs for needy students. Research shows that ten hours a week or less won't hurt grades of freshmen. For upperclassmen, the comparable figure is fifteen hours a week. Scholarships are desirable, of course. Most scholarships are small. Many companies, especially larger corporations, offer scholarships to employees' children with good grades. Trade unions, industry groups, community foundations, charitable organizations, religious establishments, and the like also offer scholarships. Merit scholarships are available for applicants with outstanding grades or talent.

In practice, however, the cost is largely met with student loans and parent loans.

The online world offers plenty of resources for learning about student loans. The mainstay federal loans include the Perkins loans, for low-income students, and Stafford loans, which come in two flavors, subsidized and unsubsidized. The federal government pays interest on subsidized Stafford loans while the student is enrolled in college. Interest and principal payments can be deferred for six months after graduation. With unsubsidized Stafford loans, interest payments accrue immediately, although principal and interest payments are deferred until six months

---

Check out the credits

The $2,500 American Opportunity Tax Credit is an expansion of the Hope Credit that will expire after 2010. But strong support exists for making it permanent. It can be claimed for all four years of college. Married couples filing jointly with a modified adjusted gross income of up to $160,000 can claim the full credit. For single filers, it's up to a MAGI of $80,000. The credit phases out for those earning above $180,000 for joint filers and $90,000 for single filers. The credit is partially refundable. A low-income family that doesn't earn enough to pay income taxes could get as much as $1,000 back. The law has a number of wrinkles. The credit is only for undergraduates going to school more than half-time. It's for qualified education expenses. To get the full benefit, the student's expenses must be $4,000 or more. You can't claim the credit for any expenses that you paid for with tax-free 529 or Coverdell money, tax-free scholarships, Pell grants, employer-provided tuition reimbursement, and the like.

The Lifetime Learning Credit is for a maximum of $2,000 for qualified educational expenses. You can claim the credit annually, with no course restrictions attached to it. The credit is for courses on the undergraduate, graduate, or professional stage. You may qualify even if you take a single class to boost your job skills. The credit is nonrefundable. It comes with income limits. You can't file for a Lifetime Credit the same year that you claim the American Opportunity Credit.

---

after graduation. Parents can take out federal PLUS loans. Parents can borrow the yearly difference between the cost of college attendance and financial aid.

Parents, I would steer clear of borrowing against your home equity to help pay for college. It's too risky a strategy. I'm not a fan of borrowing

The "private" student loan market is expanding. Parents are usually asked to cosign private student loans so that their youngster can get a better rate. The term *student loan* is misleading. They're more like high-cost credit cards than federally sponsored student loans. Private student loans are inflexible. They are potentially toxic to the student borrower. Caveat emptor.

against your retirement savings plan, either. Problem is, if you lose your job, you have six months to restore the money or you'll get hit with a 10 percent early-withdrawal penalty and pay ordinary income taxes on the amount you've withdrawn. You lose the compounding effect of your investments, too. Again, I don't think the risks are worth it.

The Loan Payment Calculus

The standard student loan repayment plan is a fixed monthly payment for ten years. How much can your student borrow? The traditional benchmark was no more than 8 percent of a college graduate's income should go toward student loans. That figure rose to 10 to 15 percent of monthly income in the 2000s. The increase was a big mistake.

The traditional benchmark is the right starting place. The higher debt-to-income ratio ignored that students often have other debts, such as car payments and credit cards. Surveys show that recent college graduates says they are feeling the strain of their debt burdens. Like all rules of thumb, the 8 percent figure should be adjusted. For example, someone earning $20,000 a year after graduation shouldn't have a total-debt-payment-to-total-income ratio that exceeds 5 percent, calculate economists Sandy Baum and Saul Schwartz in their paper "How Much Debt Is Too Much? Defining Benchmarks for Manageable Student Debt." They estimate a graduate making $40,000 a year could support a maximum ratio of 13 percent. Under no circumstances do they recommend anyone going above a 20 percent debt-to-income ratio. For most undergraduates 8 percent is a maximum. It's prudent to assume a low income in the early years after graduation.

It's easy to fall behind on student loan payments. If you think you're teetering toward default, don't hesitate. Contact your lender. Your lender doesn't want you to default any more than you do. If you are facing a short-term problem, such as unemployment, medical leave, or some other kind of economic hardship, you may qualify for deferment or forbearance. The government pays the interest on your federal loans for up to three years with deferment. The interest payments are added to the balance of the loan with forbearance.

You don't want to default. Your credit rating will be trashed. The agency that holds your loan could force your employer to deduct payments from your paycheck. The U.S. Department of Education can ask the IRS to take your tax refund if you get one and apply it to the loan. If you ever decide to return to school, you can kiss any federal student aid good-bye. Still, if you've defaulted, talk to your lender since there are ways to rehabilitate your loan. For instance, you can get out of default by making nine consecutive and on-time payments. You must negotiate the payment terms with the holder of your loan.

However, a number of other options exist for dealing with student loans. All are designed to buy you some financial relief. The options carry an important trade-off: You ease your upfront financial burden in return for raising the overall cost of your loan. Hopefully, with time your financial circumstances will improve and you'll be able to pay off the loan early. Federal student loans have no prepayment penalty. Among the major options for financial relief are:

A *graduated repayment* plan: The amount you owe increases every two to three years.

An *extended repayment* plan: It increases the length of your loan for up to twelve to thirty years. You have to pay a monthly minimum of $50.

Income contingent loan: With this loan the repayment fluctuates with your income. You don't pay much in lean years, but more when you're doing better. Whatever is left on the loan after twenty-five years is forgiven.

Income-sensitive: Your monthly loan payment is based on your annual income. The repayment period is ten years.

Income-based repayment: It uses a formula that takes into account income, family size, and your state. It's a sliding scale, but for most people their monthly payment should run at 10 percent or less of their income. The loan is forgiven after twenty-five years.

Consolidation. You take all your old student loans and repackage them into one loan. One bill. One check. You cut your monthly outlay by lengthening the life of the loan.

If Hollywood remakes the 1967 classic *The Graduate*, the advice to Benjamin might be "public service" instead of "plastics." Federal and state governments will forgive loans or make loan payments for you in certain circumstances. The military is one example. So is teaching in inner-city schools. The U.S. government will pay the remaining interest and principal on federally backed student loans for employees that have worked for the government for ten years. You must be in good standing with your student loans, too. The benefit extends to a lengthy list of other "public service" jobs, including law enforcement, public defender, nursing, and child care. It's a way to attract young talent to the public sector and public service jobs.

Ah, the halcyon days of college life. Oh, sure while you're in school the pressure of tests and research papers may have seemed burdensome. But soon after proudly taking receipt of a diploma, most grads get another document signifying their four years of education: A student loan payment book. In today's high-tech global economy, education is the stepping-stone to success. But so is being savvy about paying for that education.

CHAPTER 11

Generosity and Gratitude

We make a living by what we get. We make a life by what we give.

—Winston Churchill

THE MOST FAMOUS PERSONAL-FINANCE maven with a "don't spend more than you earn" message is Benjamin Franklin. He made his fortune publishing *Poor Richard's Almanack,* a practical annual book with all kinds of useful information from a calendar to weather predictions. It was leavened with humor and aphorisms. Many of Franklin's expressions about industry and thrift are still familiar:

Remember that time is money.

Early to bed and early to rise, makes a man healthy, wealthy, and wise.

There are no gains without pains.

He that goes a-borrowing goes a-sorrowing.

The borrower is a slave to the lender, the debtor to the creditor.

If you would be wealthy, think of saving as well as getting.

'Tis easier to suppress the first desire, than to satisfy all that follow it.

Not everyone was happy with Franklin's wisdom. Mark Twain complained that the "early to bed, early to rise" maxim had caused him much "sorrow" since his parents insisted on "experimenting on me with it."

It's too bad that the image of Franklin as a scold endures. He lived large with an astonishing career—scientist, networker, raconteur, Founding Father, ambassador to France, emissary to Britain, writer, creator of libraries and businesses. He also wrote one of the most widely read personal-finance books ever, *The Way to Wealth*, a sixteen-page pamphlet published in 1758. It was reprinted in 145 editions and seven languages during Franklin's era, according to Walter Isaacson, who wrote a biography of Franklin.

In *The Way to Wealth*, the key character is the elderly Father Abraham. He gives a speech that weaves together all of Franklin's exhortations about thrift, frugality, and industry. Franklin's advice was geared toward helping colonial Americans manage money during a time of war and taxation (the French and Indian War). But Franklin had a comic touch, too. "Poor Richard" is in the back of the room listening to Father Abraham's talk, and at the end of the speech Richard remarks, "Thus the old Gentleman ended his Harangue. The People heard it, and approved the Doctrine, and immediately practiced the Contrary, just as if it had been a common Sermon."

I like Franklin's sly humor. Even more important for our purposes, Franklin knew that savings was a means to an end, not an end in itself. His biographer Isaacson believes Franklin's real outlook on money and life is best captured by this statement in a letter to his mother: "I would rather have it said, He lived usefully, than, He died rich."

What does it mean to live usefully? It might mean having an important job that makes you a productive citizen of your community. It might mean doing public service. Or it might simply mean being a good parent. However you reckon it, what Franklin is saying is that it's not measured by how much wealth and savings you accumulate.

What I've been talking about in this book is how to think about your money in a new way: not just so many figures on a spreadsheet or so many bills in your wallet. The New Frugality is about understanding how money is connected to the rest of your life—saving and spending mindfully, not just counting dollars and cents for their own sake. From this perspective, one of the most valuable and sensible things you can do with your money is give it away.

Giving is central to managing our money. The mindfulness of giving, and the connections it forges, remind us that when you think about what matters most, it's usually relationships, experiences, and the sense of making a difference, not money and possessions. In other words, generosity and gratitude are part of the New Frugality, just as much as are thrift, planning, and discipline. When you donate to a charitable cause—it might be funding cancer research or running a soup kitchen at your local church—you're putting your money to work doing something meaningful. If you donate today, it might leave you with $100 less next week, but it's an investment in making the world a better place. That's another way of being newly frugal.

Life-Cycle Giving

Economists have developed a particular approach to financial planning (no surprise there) called life-cycle smoothing. The basic idea is that we want to maintain the highest possible standard of living throughout our lives. The practical implication is that savings isn't at the top of the personal-finance list of priorities. Spending rules. Savings is a means of supporting spending. One important part of this approach is, if you live too high on the hog early on, spending with abandon, you'll live far less well in old age. That said, if you save too much when you're younger, you'll have plenty of money in old age and a long list of regrets. "This spending of the best part of one's life earning money in order to enjoy a questionable liberty during the least valuable part of it, reminds me of the Englishman who went to India to make a fortune first, in order that he might return to England to live the life of a poet," writes Henry David Thoreau in *Walden Pond*. "He should have gone up garret at once."

Ross Levin, the Minneapolis-based CFA, is a fan of Thoreau. He took that passage to reflect on a recently retired doctor. The doctor's back went out a month after quitting work. The back problem was so severe that it completely compromised his lifestyle in retirement. "The trips that he didn't take with his family when he was working are ones that, because of physical ailments, he can't take when he is retired. How sad," wrote Levin. "What could have been done differently so he could create his family memories while the children were growing up, rather than attempting to capture them after the children had all grown?"

The answer, says Levin, is to spend your life wisely. I'm modifying his insight a bit to this: Giving is the foundation of spending your life wisely.

The Charitable Impulse

Americans have long got together to share their concerns and passions. The famous insight from Alexis de Tocqueville, the peripatetic nineteenth-century social philosopher, still resonates: "Americans of all ages, all stations of life, and all types of disposition are forever forming associations. There are not only commercial and industrial associations in which all take part, but others of a thousand different types—religious, moral, serious, futile, very general and very limited, immensely large, and very minute."

People give for all kinds of reasons. The community spirit moves people to support the arts, contribute to their alma mater, and construct low-income housing. Faith is a powerful force, with about half of all charitable contributions directed toward religious organizations. America's charities and nonprofit organizations are remarkably diverse, ranging from small groups of volunteers working out of a basement office to universities with multibillion-dollar endowments. "They are monuments to community," wrote the historian Daniel Boorstin. "They originate in the community, depend on the community, are developed by the community, serve the community, and rise and fall with the community."

Benevolence is a growth industry. The wealthy are establishing foundations at a rapid pace, with the biggest philanthropy the Bill and Melinda Gates Foundation. The wealthy haven't practiced philanthropy on this scale since the turn of the previous century, when Carnegie, Rockefeller, and other industry titans and robber barons transformed their vast fortunes into enormous charitable ventures. Yet for all the print that is lavished on the philanthropic bent of the superwealthy, community and charitable giving is dominated by ordinary people. We go to bake sales, slip coins into an outreach container at the corner deli, and reach deep into our pockets at home and at work to support all kinds of activities.

It isn't just money. Millions of Americans participate in a wide range of volunteer activities. People volunteer to mentor inner-city entrepreneurs, answer phones during a fund drive, coach recreation-league sports, and build Habitat for Humanity homes. The teenage volunteering rate has more than doubled over the past two decades, and the adult rate is up about a third over the same period.

My dad retired from the shipping business when he was seventy-four years old. He did play golf and my parents traveled. But much of his time was taken up by various community activities. He enjoyed volunteering several hours a week with the D.C. police. A more demanding job was volunteer work for the Catholic Church to get medical supplies to Cuba. The U.S. government's contentious relationship with Cuba made it critical that all the rules and regulations were carefully followed in shipping medicine. He and another aging mariner had fun with their volunteer task. My dad even visited the island's aging ports to check out their conditions for the Church. When the Bush administration cracked down on trade with Cuba in 2003, their efforts shifted to Central America.

Keep It Simple

There are plenty of sophisticated charitable-giving strategies, creatures of our byzantine tax system and complicated estate-planning rules. The jargon is impenetrable. Mistakes are costly. Thing is, the high-finance techniques are only for the wealthy with high-priced professional advisers. For the rest of us, the mantra "Keep it simple" applies.

I used to be far more haphazard in my giving. I'd be moved by a disaster, a heart-wrenching appeal, and the lure of a last-minute tax deduction. There's nothing wrong with that. But I've moved toward a more mindful approach to what I'm doing. With planning, your money will go further and have a bigger impact. Take the time to ask some basic questions, such as, Why do you want to give? What activities do you want to support? Whom do you want to help?

Once you've hit upon a mission or approach, you'll want to research the possibilities for giving. You want to assure yourself that a charity is legitimate and effective in fulfilling its mission. The Internet makes that task easier than ever. Public charities are required to make their tax returns easily available to potential donors. Every day, another charity posts this information on its Web site. You can also go to one of the online portals and charitable giving watchdog groups, such as the Better Business Bureau, the American Institute of Philanthropy, and Charity Navigator. They all promote informed giving and prize financial openness by nonprofit organizations.

Of the many options for charitable giving, here are the main ones.

Write a Check

It's easy to donate. It's how most of us give. Another highly efficient way to give money is to donate stock, mutual funds, or some other asset that has appreciated in value. In essence, you get a bigger tax break and the charity gets more money. You can also donate clothes, furniture, cars, and other goods and take a tax deduction on the gift. Make sure you get a receipt for any gifts you make.

A Will

One of the simplest steps to take is leaving money to a charity in your will. (And you should have a will anyway!) A will doesn't offer any unusual tax complications. The money you bequeath to a qualified nonprofit organization is fully deductible for federal estate-tax purposes. You can always change your mind with a will, too, and rewrite it without penalty.

You get more bang for your charitable buck by donating appreciated stock.

	CONTRIBUTE STOCK TO CHARITY	SELL STOCK AND DONATE PROCEEDS TO CHARITY
Market value of securities	$5,000	$5,000
Capital gains tax paid	$0	$450
Charitable contribution	$5,000	$4,550
Total donor tax savings	$1,650	$1,051.50

You reduce your taxes by an extra $598.50 and the charity gets an additional $450.

Note: This example assumes only federal income taxes for the 33 percent tax bracket; the federal capital gains tax is 15 percent; the stock is owned for more than one year with a cost basis of $2,000.

Charitable Gift Funds

You get to create your own family foundation on the cheap. Most donor-advised funds are run by mutual fund companies and community foundations. Depending on the institution, the minimum investment ranges between $5,000 and $50,000. The typical deal works like this: You make a contribution of cash, stock, or some other asset. You can't take the money back. You get to deduct the gift from your taxes, and you decide how to invest the money in your charitable gift fund. You recommend that the fund direct donations to the charity or charities of your choice. It's a good way to involve the whole family in giving, and it makes charitable-giving record keeping easy.

Carefully scrutinize the fees and expenses associated with these funds since they can vary significantly with more mutual fund companies and brokerage houses entering the business. (By now, you know this is a theme of mine when it comes to financial institutions.) Some financial institutions even charge a load on charitable gift funds. Ugh! You shouldn't pay a commission. Plenty of good no-load, low-fee options are available. The financial institutions that offer these funds have calculators on their Web sites for you to check out the tax benefits of your contribution.

Community foundations are regionally based donor-advised funds. They have been around for almost a century and are often among the better-known charitable institutions in any region. They direct many of the gifts they manage to charities within the local area. Indeed, a major difference between charitable gift funds and community foundations is the latter's local commitment. Like a charitable gift fund, community foundations simplify your giving. In many cases, donations can be as small as $5,000 in cash, stock, or property.

Charitable Gift Annuities

For older folks living off their income, a charitable gift annuity is a way to earn an income for the rest of your life, lower your tax bill, and support a charity. Here's the basic idea: You make a charitable gift. In return, you get a fixed lifetime payout from an annuity. The charitable tax deduction lowers your income taxes. The charity keeps the remaining principal when you die. A number of variations on this idea offer greater flexibility in return for some complexity. I'd stick with the plain-vanilla products.

The product has been around for years and it is offered by nonprofit hospitals, universities, and other well-established charities. Most states regulate it. The American Council on Gift Annuities publishes payout rates that are based on the donor's age, and most charities follow its suggestions. However, as with any financial contract it's at risk if the issuing institution runs into trouble. You can protect yourself by dealing with well-known, well-established charities with strong balance sheets and by maintaining a well-diversified portfolio.

Invest in the Community

There are other ways to put your money to work for social good. Community development banks are an underappreciated resource for investing locally. These banks offer federally insured checking, savings, and money-market deposit accounts, CDs, and other traditional banking deposits. But they also offer socially responsible funds that back loans in the community. For example, University Bank is the community development bank near where I work in St. Paul. It offers a Socially Responsible Deposit Fund (SRDF). The money goes toward supporting more affordable housing and encouraging small businesses in the St. Paul/Minneapolis area. The money is also lent to nonprofit organizations and community services in the economically challenged areas of the Twin Cities. What's the catch? There isn't one, except your deposits are used to make loans that support socially conscious projects. Most community banks offer a SRDF or something similar. (You can learn more at socialinvest.org.)

Microfinance is another intriguing giving alternative. It's essentially a system for providing small loans to poor entrepreneurs, typically self-employed and running a home-based business. Although most micro-finance institutions are started with public, philanthropic, or some other sources of money, eventually many become self-sustaining profit-making enterprises. Its modern origins date back to the mid-1970s. Among the key innovators was Nobel Peace Prize recipient Professor Muhammad Yunus of Bangladesh. He had the idea of making loans to the very poor, especially women. He started the Grameen Bank Project in 1976 and transformed it into a bank in 1983. It now has nearly eight million borrowers, 97 percent of them women. The recovery rate for loans is 98 percent, and the bank has earned a profit every year but three since its inception. Microfinance institutions have sprung up throughout Asia, Latin America, Africa, Eastern Europe, and elsewhere in the developing world. They are also found in poor American communities and elsewhere in the industrial world. Indigenous microfinance entrepreneurs have proved, with over ninety-two million customers, that the poor are bankable, contrary to conventional finance wisdom. "This is an area

where you can do good while doing well," says Brigit Helms, senior adviser at the Consultative Group to Assist the Poor. You can easily make
microfinance loans online at places like Kiva.org.

Donate Your Time

Needless to say, volunteering is an even more frugal way of giving back.
Contributing your time to an organization furthers the cause without
touching your bank balance, and as we mentioned in an earlier chapter,
it can be a great way to network and develop new skills that will serve
you in the future. Most important, it's the most direct way you can give
of yourself, and it can bring deep psychic satisfaction.

With giving, you choose to make a difference—each and every time.

A Satisfied Mind

In the aftermath of financial trauma and recession, the next decade or
more will be spent rewriting the rules of American capitalism. The process
will be messy. America's balkanized financial regulatory structure will be
overhauled and simplified. The gargantuan scale of the bailout will force a
national discussion on redefining the boundaries between the public sector and the private economy. When should companies be allowed to fail
and when should government make good on private risky bets gone bad?
How much will Washington and not Wall Street decide what sectors of the
economy get capital? How do we prevent banks and other financial institutions from privatizing profits during good times and socializing losses
in bad? Taken altogether, difficult questions like these involve what the
eighteenth-century British conservative Edmund Burke termed "one of the
finest problems in legislation, namely, to determine what the State ought
to take upon itself to direct by the public wisdom, and what it ought to
leave, with as little interference as possible, to individual exertion."

It won't be easy. My own take on the economy and society is optimistic with the passage of time. Innovation will remain the economy's driving force. So will entrepreneurial risk taking. The competitive pressures from the global economy and concerns about the rising inequality will push society and legislators toward embracing policies such as major health care and pension reform that will improve the economic security and financial welfare of Americans.

Indeed, society appears to be making one of its periodic shifts in emphasis. In broad terms, we're going from a focus on "private interests" to "public action" to use the typology of economist Albert O. Hirschman. Over the past three decades, we've lived through a period where public policy initiatives focused on open markets, open borders, deregulation, and lower taxes. The dominating idea, behind all these initiatives was that individuals promoting their own interests end up benefiting everyone. The embrace of freer-market policies enhanced economic growth after the stagnant 1970s but the losses in income and financial welfare have been large for those individuals and groups of individuals who, because of personal history and education level fell down the economic ladder even as others climbed to new heights.

Eventually every revolution breeds a counter-revolution as the neglect of certain problems accumulates. "People grow bored with selfish motives and vistas, weary of materialism as the ultimate goal. The vacation from public responsibility replenishes the national energies and recharges the national batteries," wrote the late historian Arthur Schlesinger Jr. in his essay *The Cycles of American Politics.* "A detonating issue—some problem growing in magnitude and menace beyond the capacity of the market's invisible hand to solve—at last leads to a breakthrough into a new political epoch."

The "detonating issue" was the debt gone bad and the threat of global warming. The new epoch will see families focusing on building a financial margin of safety and embracing the ethics of sustainability. The New Frugality will deeply affect how we live and work.

We all have to think about money some of the time, whether we have a lot or a little. But we all have things to be grateful for, too—whether it's a

little or a lot. Giving back to your community—whether you define that
as your neighborhood or our planet—is a way of acting on that gratitude,
and it rewards you as well. Let's give the last word to Johnny Cash:

> *Money can't buy back*
> *Your youth when you're old*
> *Or a friend when you're lonely*
> *Or a love that's grown cold*

That's the New Frugality.

Index

A Note on the Author

CHRIS FARRELL is the resident personal-finance expert and economics editor for America Public Media's *Marketplace Money*. He is also a contributing economics editor for *BusinessWeek*. Farrell has written *Right on the Money: Taking Control of Your Personal Finances,* and *Deflation: What Happens When Prices Fall?* Among Farrell's many awards are a National Magazine Award, two Loeb Awards, and the Edward R. Murrow Award. Farrell is a graduate of the London School of Economics and Stanford University. He lives in St. Paul, Minnesota.

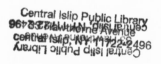